COMPUTER AND INFORMATION ETHICS

Recent Titles in
Contributions to the Study of Computer Science

Reckoners: The Prehistory of the Digital Computer, from Relays to the
Stored Program Concept, 1935–1945
Paul E. Ceruzzi

Machines and Intelligence: A Critique of Arguments Against the Possibility
of Artificial Intelligence
Stuart Goldkind

The Barefoot Expert: The Interface of Computerized Knowledge Systems
and Indigenous Knowledge Systems
Doris M. Schoenhoff

COMPUTER AND INFORMATION ETHICS

John Weckert and Douglas Adeney

Contributions to the Study of Computer Science, Number 4
G.E.Gorman, Advisory Editor

GREENWOOD PRESS
Westport, Connecticut • London

Library of Congress Cataloging-in-Publication Data

Weckert, John.
    Computer and information ethics / John Weckert and Douglas Adeney.
        p. cm.—(Contributions to the study of computer science,
    ISSN 0734–757X ; no. 4)
     Includes bibliographical references and index.
     ISBN 0–313–29362–7 (alk. paper)
     1. Computers—Moral and ethical aspects. I. Adeney, Douglas.
    II. Title. III. Series.
    QA76.9.M65W43   1997
    174´.90904—dc20   96–36528

British Library Cataloguing in Publication Data is available.

Library of Congress Catalog Card Number: 96–36528
ISBN: 0–313–29362–7
ISSN: 0734–757X

First published in 1997

Greenwood Press, 88 Post Road West, Westport, CT 06881
An imprint of Greenwood Publishing Group, Inc.

Printed in the United States of America

The paper used in this book complies with the
Permanent Paper Standard issued by the National
Information Standards Organization (Z39.48–1984).

10 9 8 7 6 5 4 3 2

Copyright Acknowledgments

The author and publisher gratefully acknowledge permission for use of the following
material:

From "Virtual Sex," by Douglas Adeney and John Weckert. *Res Publica*, September 1995.
Used with permission.

From "Censorship on the World Wide Web," by John Weckert and Douglas Adeney.
Australian Library Review 13, 1996. pp. 54–59. Used with permission.

From *The Social and Ethical Effects of the Computer Revolution* © 1996 Joseph M. Kizza
by permission of McFarland & Company, Inc., Publishers, Jefferson NC 28640.

From "Ethics, Reference Librarians and Expert Systems," by John Weckert and Stuart
Ferguson. *The Australian Library Journal*, August 1993. Used with permission.

Contents

Contents

Introduction

Information technology should provide spiritual healing, in addition to financial savings. (Brass 1995: 50)

Should censorship be applied to the Internet, and if so, what should be censored? Should computers be allowed to take the place of humans in the workforce, and in jobs of what kinds? Are people entitled to make whatever use they like of information they gain by means of their own computers, and who should have access to what information? Should employers be allowed to read the e-mail of their employees? Should computers ever be recognised as having rights? These and many related questions will be discussed in the chapters to follow. In this introduction we will begin by discussing the scope of computer and information ethics, and then outline what follows in the rest of the book.

COMPUTER AND INFORMATION ETHICS

Computer and information ethics might be (1) all of computer ethics and all of information ethics, or (2) the intersection of computer and information ethics, that is, just those issues that concern both. The domain of this book is somewhere between these two extremes. We discuss questions related to computers considered as *information processing machines*. In the rest of this section the domain of computer and information ethics will be defined and a justification given for the choice of the topics included in this book.

Is there such a thing as computer ethics, and if so, what is it? It might be argued that there is not. Any ethical problem in which computers play a role is an ethical problem regardless of the involvement of computers. Robbery with the aid of a getaway car is not seen as an issue in automobile ethics, so why for example should theft with the aid of a computer be seen as an issue in computer ethics? An ethical issue is not part of computer ethics simply because it concerns a computer. Stealing a computer is hardly an issue in computer ethics.

But there is a cluster of ethical problems around the use of computers which can legitimately be called "computer ethics." Of course it could be objected that this is completely arbitrary. We could call ethical issues surrounding the use of cars (and there are surely enough of them) "automobile ethics," or those around the use of television, "television ethics," but this is rarely done. Yet perhaps we could do this. And in some areas considered important enough, we do. In recent years a subject called environmental ethics has emerged in response to a cluster of particular concerns of growing importance. Computer ethics has emerged in the same way.

Well, if it is legitimate to talk of computer ethics, what is its domain? Which issues are issues in computer ethics and which not? Problems in computer ethics are not different or new in the sense that they are different in kind from other ethical problems, whatever that might mean. Moral philosophy has been studied systematically at least from the time of the ancient Greeks, and the ethical issues in computing are part of this tradition. What is new and different is that the development and use of computers has raised old questions in new and different ways (see Moore 1985).

In what ways are these issues different? What makes it reasonable to classify them in a domain of their own? One argument is that they are of specific concern to computer professionals qua computer professionals. They are essentially about the professional-client relationship. This is a reasonable approach. Medical ethics chiefly concerns the doctor-patient relationship. Computer professionals design and develop software and hardware for their clients to use. The important issues then include system reliability, system and data security, software theft and the like, which are typically specified in professional codes of ethics. Another approach is to include ethical issues that are raised in a unique way because of computers. For example, breaking into someone's computer account is in some ways like breaking into someone's house, but there are interesting differences. It is a logical rather than a physical entering. Unauthorised copying of software is a bit like unauthorised copying of a book, and a bit like taking a television set, but there are significant differences. There are also questions relating to work, and the loss or creation of skills, that arise in a unique way. And finally, there are questions about the creation of intelligent machines. It is this broader approach that will be taken here.

Professional ethics comprises an important part of computer ethics, but not the whole thing.

To whom is computer ethics important, or to whom should it be important? First a general comment on its importance. Many people, particularly those connected with the technical side of computing, possibly do not see it as important at all. Evidence for this is the small amount of time devoted to it in most computing and related courses in universities. But surely human beings are more than economic units to be manipulated for the economic good of their employer or even of their community. Each individual wants to lead some sort of satisfying or good life, as defined in his or her own terms. Given that most of us are gregarious to some extent, we want a society in which our lives can be more or less fulfilled. Computer and information technologies are now such a central part of our culture that ethical questions and dilemmas concerning them are unavoidable. Ethics is about human conduct, and the use and development of computer technology is part of human conduct.

Those most centrally concerned with computer and information ethics are computer and information professionals. They are the ones who either directly or indirectly are involved with end users, their clients. As such, they are in relationships something like that which a doctor has with his or her patients. These professionals are experts in various aspects of computer technology or use. But they are not just expert technologists. They are also human beings who are responsible for their actions. This is recognised by the different computing and information organisations, such as the Association for Computing Machinery, the American Library Association, and the Australian Computer Society. Professional codes of conduct have been and are still being developed. A true professional, we assume, should not only be expert in his or her field, but also have the ability and the desire to stand back and see how his or her work fits into the general realm of human affairs.

But given the scope of computer ethics outlined here, it is of concern not only to computer professionals. It is, or should be, of concern to everyone. Medical ethics is not limited to medical practitioners. Such issues as voluntary euthanasia, abortion, and in vitro fertilisation are of concern to the whole society. And so are many of the questions of computer ethics.

Now just a brief word on information ethics. The domain of information ethics comprises all of the ethical issues related to the production, storage, access, and dissemination of information. Some of these overlap with computer ethics as described above, for example, questions concerning copyright and censorship. Others do not, for example, issues to do with radio and television, and collection development in libraries. Here our concerns are only with those issues in the domain of information ethics that arise in new or interesting ways because of the role of computers in the production, storage, and so on of the information. The topics that we discuss were chosen because of their importance and interest. Questions of intellectual property, censorship, and privacy are continually raised in the popular press and are central ethical concerns in the field. The same applies to the use of computers in our working environment. Ethical worries about image manipulation, virtual reality, the use of "intelligent" systems, and the moral status of intelligent machines are raised less often, but they are gaining in both importance and interest as the technology develops. Some of the moral questions discussed have not yet arisen in practical situations, but we consider it vital that these are examined before they become urgent. Too often in the introduction of new technology moral dilemmas arise about which little thinking has been done. This has been particularly evident in the field of medical technologies. Many issues have been omitted, but we hope that by showing one way of approaching some practical ethical problems, light will be shed on how to approach those other questions as well.

STRUCTURE

In the first chapter some of the main issues in ethics are introduced, concentrating on foundational questions and beginning with those that examine the meaning of ethical or moral questions. (In this book we do as most philosophers do, using "ethical" and "moral" interchangeably.) In particular we look at objectivism, the theory that there are objective moral facts independent of any societies or people, and relativism, the view that all morality is dependent on societies or individuals. Some basic understanding of ethical theory is very valuable in the discussion of practical questions. It is also important to resist the idea that ethical judgments are "merely matters of opinion" with nothing further to be said. Matters of opinion they may be, but that does not hinder rational and in-depth discussion that can lead to agreement and useful action. Computer and information ethics as perceived here involve much more than "consciousness raising." Professional ethics are considered in the second chapter. The argument is that it is not what constitutes a profession that is important, but rather what constitutes a *professional attitude*. Anyone in almost any job can be a professional in the sense of having a professional attitude towards that job, and this attitude incorporates an ethical stance.

Computers are viewed here as information processing machines. Something is put in at one end and something else comes out at the other, or something is put in in one place and the same thing comes out in a different place. In the first case the computer is an information *processing* machine, and in the second an information *communication* machine. (Computers can of course be a combination of both.) From chapter 3 onward various important ethical topics are discussed; topics that centre around computers as information processing or communication machines. The first group of topics is concerned with the information processed or communicated, and the second with the environment created by these machines. Finally the focus turns to the machines themselves.

Chapters 3 to 8 concentrate on information related issues. The first four of these chapters (3–6) examine questions primarily concerned with the processing and transfer or communication of information. Chapters 7 and 8 focus more on information that is generated by the computer. The next two chapters, 9 and 10, look at the environment, both the real and the virtual, created by these machines. The nature of the machines is discussed in chapter 11.

Now for some more detail on the topics. Chapter 3, "Freedom, Information, and Images," begins with a brief discussion of freedom or liberty, a discussion that provides the basis for the following examination of freedom of information and the use of image manipulation. This theme of freedom is continued in chapter 4, "Censorship of the Internet." Arguments about censorship are essentially about the freedom of speech and expression. The focus is on censorship of the Internet. Chapter 5, "Intellectual Property," examines arguments about the ownership of digitally stored images, text, data, and computer software. Freedom is still an important concept here, and the central questions concern what we should be free to own or to copy. However, the most important arguments now are the narrower ones about the justifications for ownership rights. "Privacy" is both the topic and the title of chapter 6. The discussion concentrates on personal data, surveillance, and hacking.

In the next two chapters the emphasis changes a little. We move toward examining issues concerning information created by the computer. Chapter 7, "Responsibility," concentrates on accountability for software failure. It concerns the issue of who is responsible if information or other output that is generated or created, is wrong. Chapter 8, "What Computers Should Not Do," looks at the information generated by two types of computer program and examines whether computers should be used for such.

Chapter 9, "Quality of Life and Work," and chapter 10, "Virtual Reality," shift away from the information aspect to the environmental. Here the interest is in the environment created by these information processing machines. The first of these chapters considers the quality of life in "real" reality, and, in particular, working life. The second looks at what has become known as virtual reality. In chapter 11 we turn our attention to the machines themselves. Humans are, among other things, information generating and processing creatures. If machines can generate and process information in such a way that their behaviour is indistinguishable from humans, should they have the same sorts of moral rights as are commonly attributed to humans?

APPROACH

Finally, a comment on the approach taken in this book. People include many different things under the headings of "Computer Ethics" and "Information Ethics." Sometimes there is a general discussion of relevant social issues and sometimes an examination of case studies of typical situations. Or there may be an examination of more conceptual and abstract issues. Many writers take a sociological approach, others a psychological or a philosophical one, and some a mixture. Our approach is unashamedly philosophical. We are primarily concerned not only with raising, but also with analysing and arguing about various issues in computer and information ethics. Most chapters begin with a short discussion of the relevant normative ethical issues, for example, freedom or property, and then apply these to the applications. We try to argue for particular stances on issues in such a way that if you disagree with the position taken, you will at least be able to trace our line of thought and see where you think we have gone wrong. Or perhaps you will be convinced by our argument! We take this approach, not because we believe it to be the only important one, but because we believe that it is important to see these issues in the context of our ethical tradition and also that it is important to argue about them rationally and clearly.

AUDIENCE

The intended audience of this book includes those information students and professionals who work with computers, although many of the issues discussed have general application in other areas of the computing and information professions as well. While we do not discuss cases in detail, we do examine arguments and adopt positions. It is our hope that this approach assists students and professionals to better understand the moral questions of their profession, helps them to make the most appropriate ethical decisions, and above all, enables them to adopt a professional attitude. Where possible and appropriate, we link our discussions with the appropriate parts of relevant codes of ethics.

This book is suitable for a one-semester course for computing, library, or other information students. Information professionals can also use it as a means of coming to grips with the important moral issues they face.

REFERENCES

Brass, Charles. 1995. Virtual spirituality. *Information Age* [Melbourne, Australia] (September): 50.

Moore, James H. 1985. What is computer ethics? *Metaphilosophy* 16: 266–75.

FURTHER READING

Dejoie, Roy, George Fowler, and David Paradice. 1991. *Ethical Issues in Information Systems*. Boston: Boyd & Fraser.

Forester, Tom, and Perry Morrison. 1995. *Computer Ethics: Cautionary Tales and Ethical Dilemmas in Computing*. 2d ed. Cambridge, MA: MIT Press.

Johnson, Deborah G. 1994. *Computer Ethics*. 2d ed. Englewood Cliffs, NJ: Prentice Hall.

Johnson, Deborah G., and Helen F. Nissenbaum, eds. 1994. *Computers, Ethics and Social Values*. Englewood Cliffs, NJ: Prentice Hall.

Kizza, Joseph M., ed. 1994. *Ethics in the Computer Age: Conference Proceedings, Gatlinburg, Tennessee, November 11–13, 1994*. New York: Association for Computing Machinery.

Kizza, Joseph M., ed. 1996. *The Social and Ethical Issues of the Computer Revolution*. Jefferson, NC: McFarland and Company.

McFarland, Michael C. 1990. Urgency of ethical standards intensifies in computer community. *Computer* 23 (March): 77–81.

Oz, Effy. 1994. *Ethics for the Information Age*. [no place]: Business and Educational Technologies.

Tavani, Herman T. 1995. A computer ethics bibliography. *Computers and Society* 25 (June): 8–18; (September): 27–37; (December): 9–38.

The Meaning of Ethics

The boundaries of the study called Ethics are variously and often vaguely
conceived: but they will perhaps be sufficiently defined, at the outset, for the
purposes of the present treatise, if a "Method of Ethics" is explained to mean
any rational procedure by which we determine what individual human beings
"ought"—or what it is "right" for them—to do, or to seek to realise by voluntary means. (Sidgwick 1874: 1)

Ethics is about how we live, and particularly about how we live in relation
to others. Sometimes when we speak of ethics we are speaking about sets
of rules, or codes, that govern or guide our conduct. At other times we are
speaking of a study of or inquiry into how we ought to live and to conduct
ourselves. This book is concerned with both matters, although primarily
with aspects of the latter. The first is important because professional
bodies often have codes of ethics or codes of conduct that their members
are supposed to follow. The second is important because it is here that we
must face difficult issues and try to work out for ourselves how we ought
to act toward our fellow human beings, or perhaps toward all sentient or
intelligent beings, or perhaps toward further things as well.

In this first chapter we consider some of the main theories of ethics, and
try to show how the more theoretical and the more applied aspects relate.
In the next we look at what it is to be a professional, and the role that ethics
should have for the professional.

This chapter is perhaps the most challenging in the book, which is probably not a good thing for a first chapter, but it contains general material of

importance. Discussion of practical ethical questions frequently leads to the questioning of the foundations of our moral judgements. The issues considered here help to provide a framework for answering those questions. After a general introduction we consider some of the main ethical theories, which we classify as either objectivist or relativist. We then outline several objectivist views and raise two general difficulties for them, which we call the Diversity Problem and the Verification Problem, and then turn to relativism. Here we encounter two versions, cultural relativism and subjectivism. After an explanation of the cultural version and a look at the problem of the individual dissenter, we focus attention on subjectivism and on three common objections to it.

You will notice that all of the theories mentioned here have problems. Unfortunately, that's life! Just as in the more theoretical parts of science, we must accept the theory that seems to be the best available given the current state of our understanding. Luckily, however, these different ethical theories do not always lead to different positions on practical issues. For example, the two authors of this book disagree about the basis of morals; one is a subjectivist and the other an objectivist. But on the practical issues discussed here we are largely in agreement. By the end of this chapter we shall see how this is possible.

OBJECTIVISM AND RELATIVISM

In the opening paragraph of the Introduction we raised a number of ethical questions concerning computers, and we will be discussing them and many others in the course of this book. You, the reader, may well have thought and talked about many such questions yourself. But you may also have noticed that discussions of ethical questions usually do not get very far before people wonder, or voice an opinion, about the status or meaning of ethics itself. When we say that something is right or wrong, good or bad, what are we saying about it? If you and I disagree on some ethical question, what exactly are we disagreeing about? Consider for example hacking—gaining unauthorised access via a computer to information that is supposed to be secret. Suppose that you say that it is morally wrong and I say that it is not. What is the point at issue between us? On what do we disagree? It is obviously not a matter of whether hacking is illegal, for we may agree that it is, or is not, as the case may be. Moreover, one may well believe that certain activities are illegal but not immoral, or vice versa. For example, in some places homosexuality between consenting adults in private is illegal, but many would deny that it is immoral. Many would also hold that copying certain software is not immoral, even if illegal; for example, copying games for personal use, when one would never consider buying them. Lying, on the other hand, is generally regarded as immoral but is hardly anywhere illegal, except in certain contexts, such as law courts. And many would see racial vilification on the Internet as immoral, but it is not illegal yet in most places. So what *do* we mean when we say that something is morally right or wrong, good or bad?

This is a hugely controversial question in philosophy, and many a volume has been written on it. We shall attempt a very simple sketch of some of the main theories, classified into two main varieties often called *objectivist* and *relativist*.

Objectivism

Objectivists believe that there are moral truths, which hold good independently of what we like or dislike. Just as it is true, whether we like it or not, that the sun is larger than the moon and that humans require oxygen to survive, so it is true that certain acts are right and certain others are wrong. If you and I disagree morally over some act, then at least one of us is mistaken, ignorant of, or in some way blind to the moral fact in question. (In some cases of course we might both be mistaken.) For many objectivists, moral knowledge may be as secure as knowledge of any other kind. An objectivist philosopher we know once declared, when speaking of the American serial murderer and cannibal Jeffrey Dahmer, that if he knew anything at all he knew that what Dahmer did was wrong. It is important not to confuse objectivism with *absolutism*. An absolutist holds that actions of certain kinds (e.g., killing, software copying) are always wrong, no matter what the circumstances may be. Paradoxical though this may at first sound, there are actually degrees of absolutism, in the sense that the category of actions held to be always wrong (or right) may be more or less wide; one absolutist may say that killing a human being is always wrong, while a more general one may say that killing any sentient being, that is, anything that can think and feel, is always wrong, and an even more general one may say that killing anything at all is always wrong. In the case of software copying, some may say that all copying is wrong, and others that it is wrong only in cases where vendors miss out on a sale. Moving in the direction of the specific rather than the general, we may find someone taking the common view that killing humans is permissible in some circumstances but not in others. Suppose such a person holds that certain cases of self-defence are the only cases in which homicide is permissible. Such a person could then be said to be an absolutist with respect to capital punishment, euthanasia, and so on: They are always wrong. What about permissible and impermissible killing in self-defence? If our friend is able to be specific here and say, "Killing in self-defence is sometimes allowable, but is always wrong when . . ." then he or she could still technically count as an absolutist with respect to the latter cases, but the term "absolutist" is normally taken to mean someone whose principles are comparatively general. And objectivists are not at all committed to being absolutists in such a sense. Many are, but they need not be. An objectivist might hold that killing a human being is permissible only in certain circumstances, which might be very carefully specified, and be similarly specific with respect to other kinds of behaviour such as truth telling, business dealings, electronic surveillance, and so on. The distinguishing feature of the objectivist is not absolutism of any sort, but the belief in moral facts of which we can somehow have knowledge.

Of what sort are these moral facts, and how do we come to know them? What fact is expressed in a moral judgement of the form "Action X is morally right"? Objectivists give various answers, of which some of the most popular go somewhat as follows:

1. Action X promotes, or best promotes, some end such as the sum total of human happiness, or social harmony, or perhaps the survival of the species. Because "right" is here defined in terms of something natural, in the sense of being observable by ordinary means in the world around us, such a view is often called *naturalism*.

2. Action X's rightness is a special moral quality that cannot be defined in terms of happiness or harmony or survival or anything at all. We perceive such qualities by means of a special faculty, sometimes called intuition. This view is called *intuitionism*.

3. Action X is commanded, or at least approved, by God. This is known as the *divine command theory*.

4. Action X is what any rational person would do in the appropriate circumstances. We may call this, with caution, *rationalism*. We say "with caution," because philosophical views of many other types have been given this name.

Other answers have been offered, and so have numerous variations on these four examples. But as outlined here they are quite representative. They face respectively, like many philosophical views, all sorts of objections, but we shall confine ourselves here to two general and related ones, which may be called the Diversity Problem and the Verification Problem. Each of them seems to affect, in its own way, each of the above four versions of objectivism.

The Diversity Problem is this: If moral facts (of whatever kind they may be) are there to be seen (by whatever means), why is there not much greater agreement on them among societies, from period to period in the same society, and among groups and individuals in the same society at the same time? Some societies morally approve of female genital mutilation, and some condemn it; our ancestors happily practised slavery, and we condemn it; many people in our society at present morally endorse abortion while many oppose it, and so on. How is all this moral diversity to be explained? Why do so many societies and groups and individuals have defective means of perceiving moral truths, which it seems must be the case? The problem arises for any form of objectivism, but perhaps most acutely for the divine command version: Why does a God who cares about us and wants us to act well allow so many of us to be mistaken as to his attitude (whatever it may be) to abortion, artificial contraception, women priests, euthanasia, capital punishment, war, and so on?

This all raises the Verification Problem. If other societies' moral views differ from ours, or other individuals' differ from mine, or even if we can imagine them differing, how can it be shown that ours, or mine, are correct? Let us see how this applies specifically to each version of objectivism in turn. It affects version (1), naturalism, as follows: How are we to be sure that X will best promote, or is even the option most likely to promote, happiness or harmony? Perhaps there is some scope for solid evidence and demonstration here, but consider (2), intuitionism: it may well be the case that my intuition tells me very definitely that X is right, but yours tells you with equal assurance that X is wrong. Whose intuition is correct and whose in error? I may have the majority on my side, but are majority opinions always correct? How could our dispute be satisfactorily settled? And of course the problem clearly arises for view (3), the divine command theory. The man who assassinated Israeli Prime Minister Yitzhak Rabin in 1995 claimed that he was acting on God's orders. If he was sincere about this, how are we to be sure that he was mistaken? God did after all command Abraham to kill another Isaac (Gen. 22), and even in the New Testament we find Jesus saying that he has come to bring not peace but a sword (Matt. 10). What about view (4), the rationalist one? Rational people may, it seems, behave in all sorts of ways, with all sorts of goals; why is it more rational to be sharing and fair, say, than to be selfish? Why is it not rational to harm others for one's own benefit, especially when there is good reason to think that one can get away with it? Philosophers have often tried to show that unselfishness, honesty, and so on are rational, but consider the words of David Hume: "Tis not contrary to reason to prefer the destruction of the whole world to the scratching of my finger" (1749: 416, Section II. III. III). We may well call such a preference unreasonable, but what does this mean? Do we mean, and could we show, that there is some defect in such a preferrer's deductive powers, or consistency, or clarity of thought, or any other aspect of being a rational person? Perhaps by "unreasonable" here we mean only that such a preference is not what it ought to be. However, if by a "rational person" we do mean, at least in part, "one who makes morally right choices," then view (4) comes down to the claim that "Action X is morally right" means "Action X is what a person who makes morally right choices would do," which does not tell us much about the meaning of "morally right."

The authors of this book actually disagree as to how serious the Diversity Problem and the Verification Problem are for objectivists. One of us thinks that diversity is hard for the latter to explain, while the other sees moral agreement as plentiful and more significant. Virtually everyone is appalled by the behaviour of Jeffrey Dahmer, and by the 1996 massacres in Dunblane, Scotland, and Port Arthur, Australia. Does this level of agreement suggest that we may, after all, talk here of moral knowledge? But what of the Verification Problem? One of us concedes that it is difficult or even impossible to verify conclusively that some moral position is the correct one. But, he asks, so what? We live with this continually in the sciences, but few of us reject the objectivity of science. We believe that there is a world out there independent of us, even though we cannot be sure that our beliefs about much of it are true, at least at the more theoretical level. Most do not doubt that there is some truth about the beginning of the universe, but there is probably no way to conclusively verify which theory is the correct one. The fact that there are differences of opinion and that it is not easy to know how to show which is the right one, does not imply that there is no right one. And this is just as true of ethical questions as of scientific ones. The other author says that the position in morality is more serious than this, because important questions of action and policy depend on beliefs that are hotly disputed. Suppose that we are on different sides of some ethical question, and that there is no more independent reason or evidence for one side than for the other. That is, my position is no more and no less supportable than yours. If I act on my view, how well based is my conduct? And it should be well based because it may have very serious consequences for you and for others.

Relativism

Let us now turn to relativism, and ask what it says and how it fares. Two main varieties of it may be distinguished. One of them, *cultural relativism*, holds that moral values are relative to the particular culture or society that accepts them: Not only do they differ from one culture or society to another, but each such value is simply a matter of what its culture happens to approve or forbid and we cannot say that one culture's values are superior to, or more correct than, another's. A given practice may be morally approved of in one culture and forbidden in another, and we cannot say that either culture has the truth, because there is no truth to be had. Their values are just different, and that is that.

The point is not simply that different societies may find themselves in different circumstances, and develop different practices accordingly. It is often reported that in traditional Eskimo tribal life, where conditions were so harsh that subsistence was a real battle, the unproductive elderly were expected to commit suicide by walking off into the snow; things are different in our society, where they are maintained, at public expense if need be (though they are sometimes shunted off into nursing homes, which some see as a fate worse than the Eskimo one). But the difference between the practices of the two cultures may well depend upon the difference in our material circumstances; if we lived in a situation as tough as theirs, where attempting to carry "passengers" would endanger the lives of all, then we would quite possibly, albeit reluctantly, develop a similar practice and expect compliance with it. More to the point, we may now concede that if we were to get into such a situation, such a practice would be morally in order. So although there is certainly a difference between their former practice and our current one, and this difference seems to be in a clear sense relative to (i.e., dependent upon) our different circumstances, there is really no essential difference between our moral values; we could agree with those former Eskimos that the survival of the unproductive elderly is desirable but the survival of the rest of the group is more important and is to be preferred in situations where, unfortunately, we cannot have both.

Rather, the cultural relativist claims that moral values differ in a more fundamental way from one society or culture to another. Female genital mutilation, for example, is abhorred in our society but favoured and practised in certain African ones, while slavery has been seen as a good thing by many societies but is certainly not so regarded by ours. And these differences do not rest upon differences in our circumstances in the way that the one in the Eskimo case did; we do not say that if we were in those African societies' situation, then female genital mutilation would be all right, or that if slavery allowed certain classes in our society to live more comfortably, as it has done where practised, then that would be all right too. It may well be true that slavery would do that for us, but we do not consider that to be any sort of an argument for it. The moral differences between those societies and ours on these matters do not depend on differences in circumstances, but depend on, or are manifestations of, differences between sexually or otherwise inegalitarian societies on the one hand and our comparatively egalitarian one on the other. At least officially, we oppose the suffering of women as much as that of men, and agree with one person's right to freedom in employment and ownership of his or her life as much as any other's. In the computing field, some of the world's larger countries have radically different views on the copying of software. These differences too, it could plausibly be argued, stem not from differences in circumstance (one country is much more affluent than the other), but in fundamental differences in attitudes toward private property. One emphasises individualism and the other collectivism.

So the relativist stresses the existence of moral diversity, and sees much of it as irreducibly, fundamentally, moral. But of course he or she adds a further claim—that one culture or society's values cannot by any objective criterion be deemed better, or more correct, than another's. These two claims are clearly different, though they are sometimes rolled up together in such a statement as "What's right in one society may be wrong in another." As anti-relativists, that is objectivists, are quick to point out, if this means merely that what is thought right in one society may be thought wrong in another, then it is obviously true. But if what it means is that what actually *is* right in one society may be wrong in another, then that is quite a different claim and according to those anti-relativists, false, unless we are referring to the relevance of circumstances as in the Eskimo case above. If it is not a matter of different circumstances, they say, then one of the societies has simply got things wrong: It is mistaken on a moral matter of fact. This of course raises the Verification Problem, but anti-relativists are at least correct in pointing out that the first of the relativist's claims does not prove the second—the existence of fundamental moral diversity does not prove that no moral standards are better than any others.

Fair enough, the relativist may reply, but does not the existence of such diversity at least lend cultural relativism great support? The reality of diversity suggests that, rather than morality being a body of facts perceivable by us in some way (which should cause much greater agreement than we actually find), it is much more likely to be a matter of likes and dislikes, tastes and aversions, passed on in a social group and reinforced by rewards and penalties, than a matter of perceiving facts that are supposed to hold good irrespective of those likes and dislikes.

As noted above, there is room for disagreement over the significance of diversity. Yet, whatever support cultural relativism gains here, it has some serious problems. One of them is simply this: If moral values are relative to whole cultures or societies (these notions differ, but that is not important here), where does that leave an individual moral dissenter? Suppose a given society sees slavery as morally permissible. And suppose some dissenting member of that society thinks that slavery is wrong. Can this make sense, on the cultural relativist view? On that view, to say that it is wrong is to say that one's society disapproves of it—and so if one knows that one's society does not disapprove of it, one cannot say it is wrong. And this is an absurd consequence of cultural relativism. Dissenting from attitudes prevailing in one's society may bring unpopularity or even danger, but it is not, as such, incoherent or paradoxical. On some matters, such as slavery, those who dissented from the formerly prevailing attitude and promoted reform are certainly not now seen as confused or ignorant about the meaning of morality.

And so we come to the second main variety of moral relativism. Our moral judgements express not our society's or our culture's approvals and disapprovals, it is said, but our own. When I say that some practice is morally wrong I am essentially expressing not my society's disapproval, but my own. My society's may well agree with mine, and may indeed have contributed largely to its formation, via my parents or in other ways, but it is not my ultimate reference point, and on some matters I may actually be at odds with it: The people who have taught me or made some impression on me, including perhaps my freethinking parents, the books I have read, the experiences I have had, may have shaped me into a dissenter or even a crusading reformer. The view that my moral judgements express my own likes and dislikes may be called individual relativism, but is more often known as *subjectivism*. If you say censoring the Internet is right and I say it is wrong, then, says the subjectivist, you are expressing your liking for such a practice and I am expressing my aversion, and there is no objective measure by which it could be said that either of us is correct or mistaken. We just have what is sometimes called a "disagreement in attitude" and that is that.

We noted earlier that objectivist views face many objections, though we discussed just two. There is no shortage of challenges to subjectivism either. We will consider three that are closely related.

First, there is what may be called the Irrationality Objection. If morality is just a matter of taste, it is said, this leaves no room for rationality—for the important place of reason in our moral choices. We expect rationality in others' moral judgements and in our own, and rightly so, for morality is one of the noblest of the attributes of our distinctively, or at least supremely, rational species. Subjectivism, by seeing morality as merely a matter of likes and dislikes, desires and aversions, is both offensive and misconceived.

Next, there is the Arbitrariness Objection: We may like one thing or action and dislike another, but if there is no reason that shows why the former is in fact better than the latter, then our choice of the former is essentially arbitrary. We may prefer to be compassionate toward our fellows rather than ruthlessly exploitative, but why not opt for the reverse?

Third, we have the Triviality Objection. How can we take morality seriously as we do, and as we ought to do, if it is what the subjectivist says it is? Likes and dislikes, desires and aversions, are essentially trivial: The subjectivist sees morality as if it were similar to having a taste for dark chocolate rather than milk, or for television situation comedies rather than game shows. And this is another insult to morality and to those who take it seriously.

These objections are all commonly raised, in various forms, but it seems to one of us that they are easily met. First, the Irrationality Objection. May not our desires and aversions, or many of them, be subject to rational support and appraisal? I may say that I want a certain political party to be elected, or that I dislike a certain policy being pursued by my university, or that I prefer one computer to another, and in each case it would be quite in order for someone to ask me why, and unsatisfactory on my part if I could give no reason. The reasons I give might themselves be queried, of course, in various ways. Suppose I say that computer A is a little less versatile than computer B but much more trouble free, and so I prefer A. I might be asked to support my claim that A is a little less versatile, or that it is more trouble free; alternatively, or additionally, I might be asked why I prefer the much more reliable to the slightly more versatile. And I may be able to answer; in the latter case, perhaps this will be in terms of the comparative importance to me of avoiding frustration and loss of time and data. If the questioning continues, and I am asked why such things are so important to me, then I may be near the point of having to say, "Look, they just are, all right?" So perhaps we cannot give reasons for all our desires and aversions, likes and dislikes, and to demand them would be to demand the infinite regress of desiring or liking one thing because of something else, and that thing because of something further, and that thing because of something else again, and so on. But many of our desires, preferences, likes, and so on are certainly amenable to reasoning, and indeed are expected to be. And why should the same not hold for morality? We may have, and have to have, some ultimate values for which we cannot give reasons, but below this level, as it were, there may be plenty of scope for rationality. A subjectivist may say that he or she thinks bomb-making instructions on the Internet are bad (i.e., prefers them not to exist) because of their potential to cause suffering, even though it is hard to give a reason for being averse to causing suffering.

What about the Arbitrariness Objection? This one should not trouble the subjectivist either. I may not be able to give a reason for preferring X to Y, but may strongly prefer X nonetheless, so that my choice of it on any given occasion does not seem arbitrary to me at all. I may arbitrarily choose one biscuit on the plate rather than its neighbour, but I do not *arbitrarily* choose to return a dropped purse to its owner rather than pocket it, or to respect children rather than murder them, or to oppose censorship rather than support it, or to support the control of computer viruses rather than their proliferation. It may be true that, but for my heredity or my environment or both, I may have turned out to be a thief or a murderer or a creator of computer viruses, but the fact is that I did not, and my choices to act otherwise express the character I actually have. Such choices, many of which I do not think about consciously, let alone deliberate on, are not at all like the above choice of the biscuit. Of course even a biscuit choice may well be non-arbitrary despite the fact that the nature of your taste buds or your early childhood experiences or whatever could quite imaginably have caused you to have the opposite preference. You unhesitatingly choose the fruit biscuit because you love those and dislike cream ones.

Someone might be unhappy about the deterministic suggestion here that we are entirely the products of causal factors in our heredity or environment or both. And this is understandable, but fortunately need not distract us. The fact is that many of our choices are made in accordance with clear and settled preferences—however we came to acquire those prefer-ences—and so are not at all arbitrary. And there is no reason why the sub-jectivist cannot say that such choices include our moral ones, except perhaps those where a moral decision is a "line ball" and we go for one al-ternative without any confidence that it is the better choice. But even here it is not as though it does not matter which option we choose. It does mat-ter, but the choice is just very difficult.

Then there is the Triviality Objection; how will this be answered? Many of our desires and aversions and preferences are quite trivial, but many are certainly not, and the subjectivist may hold that our moral ones are among our most important. This invites, however, a further question. We have many desires, aversions, and preferences, including many strong ones, that we do not see as matters of morality. You might have a prefer-ence for dark chocolate over milk, for example, a desire to backpack around Australia, or an aversion to babies. These preferences or aversions could have moral significance for you—you might object to foods con-taining milk, as a product involving the exploitation of animals, or you might have promised your late parent that you would do the backpack-ing, or you might regard babies as morally reprehensible for their noise and mess—but they would probably not. You may just like dark chocolate more, or desire adventure, or be irritated by babies without morally blam-ing them. So what is it that distinguishes our moral desires and so on from our nonmoral ones? When is a preference a moral preference?

This question has been answered in many ways, which could be set out and discussed at length, but we cannot do this here. Subjectivists often say, however, that our moral preferences are those that are in some partic-ular way important to us in the way we organise and reflect upon our lives, and in the way we think about the lives of others. Different subjec-tivists offer different accounts of the kind of importance in question, but many of them do clearly take care of the Triviality Objection. It may be sufficient to note here that many of our preferences in life do obviously have special importance of some kind; the subjectivist may hold that one such kind defines morality. And so when we ask whether or when elec-tronic surveillance or breach of copyright or censorship of the Internet is right or wrong, we are trying to reach a stance on such issues, with thought that may be very rational and serious, in the light of our impor-tant preferences of the appropriate kind.

THREE LEVELS OF ETHICAL THINKING

The debate over the meaning or status of morality has gone on for a very long time and is still very much alive. With such fundamental dis-agreements between objectivists and relativists (as shown in Figure 1.1), and among objectivists of various sorts and among relativists of various

Figure 1.1
Summary of Ethical Theories and Objections Raised

Types of Theory	Versions	Difficulties
Objectivism	Naturalism	Diversity and Verification problems
	Intuitionism	Diversity and Verification problems
	Divine command	Diversity and Verification problems
	Rationalism	Diversity and Verification problems
Relativism	Cultural relativism	Dissenter problem
	Subjectivism	Irrationality objection
		Arbitrariness objection
		Triviality objection

sorts, what hope is there of meaningful discussion of the difficult ethical questions arising in war or politics or sexuality or reproductive technology or computing or information? If you and I cannot agree on what ethics is fundamentally about, how can we hope to agree in our ethical judgements on the above matters and others? The answer, perhaps surprisingly, is that there is probably about as good a chance of our agreeing as there would be if we were both subjectivists or both objectivists. Suppose in fact that you are a subjectivist and I am an objectivist of type (2), an intuitionist. We disagree then in what is known as *meta-ethics*, the study or topic of what moral judgements mean or what job they do. But we may find ourselves agreeing solidly in *normative ethics*, which consists of particular judgements and principles. For instance, the subjectivist and objectivist may agree that the ultimate standard of right and wrong is *utility*, that is, "the greatest happiness of the greatest number"; despite their meta-ethical difference they are both utilitarians, and may work together to do and promote those actions that are most likely to bring about the greatest possible happiness or satisfaction for the largest possible number of people. (Utilitarianism will be discussed further in chapter 3.) For me, the intuitionist, this is ordained by a moral fact perceived by a special intellectual faculty; for you, the subjectivist, it is just a matter of a desire of some special sort, but this is no bar to our normative ethical harmony. (This is why it is a mistake to think of utilitarianism as a theory competing with objectivism and subjectivism; it is compatible with either, being a normative ethical theory while they are meta-ethical theories.) Further, the objectivist and subjectivist may quite possibly agree not only in their general meta-ethical principle(s), but in the particular judgements that appeal partly to them and partly to other things such as estimates of consequences. They may both, for example, oppose capital punishment, electronic surveillance, and software copyrighting, believing that all things considered and in the long run the general happiness is best served by such policies. As a matter of fact, as we have admitted already, we two authors do disagree in meta-ethics; one of us is an objectivist, and the other a subjectivist. Yet we agree on many issues in normative ethics, including many of those raised in this book.

On the other hand, being on the same side in meta-ethics is no guarantee of agreement in normative ethics. Suppose that you and I are both objectivists of the intuitionist variety. Your intuition may tell you one thing when it comes to intellectual property or cyberporn or whatever, and mine may tell me something quite different. If we are both subjectivists then your desires may very well conflict with mine on such matters, and so again we have a normative ethical disagreement.

And so: Although normative discussions of ethical issues in computing and elsewhere often lead quickly to the raising of meta-ethical issues, it is possible to a very great extent to discuss those normative questions without reference to the meta-ethical ones. We may talk about censorship and privacy and so on, giving reasons for our positions (reasons that may or may not appeal to utilitarianism), and assessing others' positions and their reasons for them, largely independently of meta-ethical debates. We say "largely" here because some meta-ethical differences between us may make some difference to our normative views. If you are a divine command theorist, for example, you are more likely to think that we should keep the Sabbath (whenever it is) holy than if you are not. But in practice many objectivists and many subjectivists talk to one another quite productively on normative issues, and reach happy agreement on them.

There are actually three levels of ethical thinking and debate that we may usefully distinguish, and the relationships among them are quite open, as illustrated in Figure 1.2. First, there is the level of meta-ethics, where for the sake of simplicity we have chosen intuitionism and subjectivism as our examples. Next, there is the level of general normative stances. Utilitarianism is a good example here, contrasted with *pluralism*— the view that our ethical duties cannot be reduced to a single fundamental one, perhaps encapsulated in some version of the principle of utility, but rather that there are several. Pluralists say that such things as honesty, truth telling, fidelity to one's promises, and so on, are ethical demands quite independent of, and sometimes competing with, the value of utility. Sometimes, for example, we should keep a promise or tell the truth even when we could make more of a contribution to the general happiness by breaking the promise or lying. Third, there is the level of particular issues, such as censorship of the Internet: One might be for it or against it. (Of course one might be for some uses of censorship and against others, in

Figure 1.2
The Three Levels of Ethical Thinking

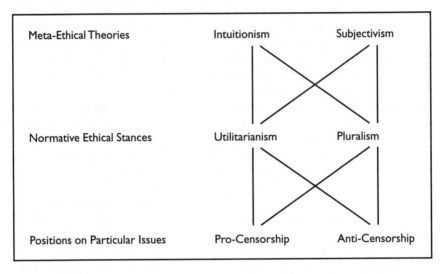

Meta-Ethical Theories	Intuitionism	Subjectivism
Normative Ethical Stances	Utilitarianism	Pluralism
Positions on Particular Issues	Pro-Censorship	Anti-Censorship

which case the third level on our table could be expressed more precisely, but we may keep things simple to illustrate our main point.)

The relationships between each level and the adjacent one are open in the following way. If you are an intuitionist you might be either a utilitarian or a pluralist, depending on what your intuitions tell you; and if you are a subjectivist you might again be either a utilitarian or a pluralist, depending on whether you have a single fundamental desire of the appropriate kind for something like the greatest happiness of the greatest number, or a plurality of desires, not reducible to one, that may have to be chosen between in cases (rare, one hopes) of conflict. And so either theory at the top level is compatible with either stance at the middle level.

Now, when we consider the relationship between the middle level and the bottom one, we find that a similar situation holds. If you are a utilitarian you will favour censorship if you believe that it will best serve, all things considered, the general happiness; you will oppose censorship if you believe that it will be ineffective and a waste of effort, or that the pleasures prevented by censorship are legitimate and greater than any harm prevented. On the other hand, if you are a pluralist you might also be either for or against censorship. You may be for it if you think that on balance it saves significant harm, for even a pluralist is likely to agree that the general happiness is a very important consideration, even if not the only important one. Or you may be against censorship if you hold that, apart from the question of its utility, it is objectionable because the free expression of tastes and opinions is a crucial aspect of human liberty and individuality, which are good things in themselves.

Numerous other moves and arguments are possible within this framework, but we hope that enough has been said to show the openness in the relationships among the three levels of ethical thinking and the importance of keeping them distinct in one's mind. In the remainder of this book we shall not actually concern ourselves any further with the top level, the level of meta-ethics. We have gone into it at some length because so many people discussing normative issues do quickly find themselves raising or facing meta-issues, which are of interest and importance for their own sakes, and of which some understanding is useful if only for appreciation of the openness claimed above. Now since this book is to be about particular issues including censorship, should we similarly stop talking about utilitarianism and pluralism?

No, we should not stop talking about them, for the relationship between the middle level and the bottom one—between our general normative stance and our judgements on particular issues—is importantly different from the relationship between the top two levels. Despite the openness between the middle and bottom levels, when discussing particular issues such as censorship we frequently appeal, and find others appealing, to general normative stances of a utilitarian or anti-utilitarian kind. We shall encounter many such appeals on various topics as we investigate the field of computer and information ethics.

SUMMARY

In this chapter we have introduced some important concepts and theories of ethics. Among these are four varieties of objectivism and two of relativism, with various objections and possible replies. We have concluded by distinguishing this level of moral thinking—meta-ethics—from two others, normative stances and positions on particular issues.

REFERENCES

Hume, David. 1739. *Treatise of Human Nature*; page citations to the edition of Selby-Bigge, 1975.
Sidgwick, Henry. 1874. *The Methods of Ethics*; page citation to the 1966 edition, New York: Dover Publications.

FURTHER READING

Grassian, Victor. 1981. *Moral Reasoning: Ethical Theory and Some Contemporary Moral Problems*. Englewood Cliffs, NJ: Prentice Hall.
Mackie, J. L. 1977. *Ethics: Inventing Right and Wrong*. Harmondsworth: Penguin Books.

Mill, John Stuart. 1863. *Utilitarianism*; edition of Sokar Piest, 1957.
Piest, Sokar, ed. 1957. *John Stuart Mill: Utilitarianism*. New York: Liberal Arts Press.
Rachels, James. 1986. *The Elements of Moral Philosophy*. New York: Random House.
Singer, Peter. 1993. *How Are We to Live? Ethics in an Age of Self-Interest*. Melbourne: Text Publishing Company.
Singer, Peter, ed. 1994. *Ethics*. Oxford: Oxford University Press.

2

Professional Ethics

Without professionalization, experts are essentially guns for hire. (Johnson and Mulvey 1995: 63)

The territory of normative ethics is large, and often divided into fields such as business ethics, research ethics, political ethics, educational ethics, biomedical ethics, computer ethics, and so on. Each of these comprises ethical issues and principles pertaining to a particular sector of life, though they may of course overlap: A given issue may for example be both one of research ethics and one of computer ethics. Now many people who make a living out of working with computers or with information think of themselves as, or would be described by others as, professionals, and as such they may be seen by themselves and others as subject to something called professional ethics. What is this field, to whom is it relevant, and how? It will be useful to distinguish two senses of the word "profession."

THE BROAD SENSE OF "PROFESSION"

In this sense a profession is anything done for a living: A professional golfer or carpenter is one who makes a living out of playing golf or doing carpentry, as distinct from the amateur, who seeks no such reward but pursues the activity just for the love of it. People who have certain occupations, like various other roles in life, are subject to certain rights and responsibilities applying to those occupations and not to others, or at least not to all others. A doctor has a duty of confidentiality that does not apply in the same way to a police officer, but they both have the ethical and legal obligation to be sober at work, unlike for example a freelance writer whose best work may not be done under the influence, but perhaps it is, and in any case most people would see this as an issue of prudence rather than morality. And of course people of certain occupations have ethical responsibilities not applicable to people of certain others. Examiners' obligation to assess students fairly, for example, could not apply to non-examiners, people who do not assess students at all. The Association for Computing Machinery (ACM) Code of Ethics and Professional Conduct lists a number of ethical principles that apply outside the world of computing, but perhaps especially acutely within it because of the technology available to members: They should for example "honor property rights including copyrights and patents" (1.5), "give proper credit for intellectual property" (1.6), and "respect the privacy of others" (1.7). Likewise the Australian Computer Society (ACS) Code of Ethics states that members should "endeavour to preserve the integrity and security of others' information" (1.2), and "respect the proprietary nature of others' information" (1.3), and in a similar vein the American Library Association (ALA) Code of Ethics states, "We recognize and respect intellectual property rights" (IV).

In some cases, of course, ethical values recognised by people of a certain occupation may conflict with ones more generally recognised. Professional pickpockets (unless they are conscience-stricken ones) think it is morally in order to pick pockets, whereas most of us think it out of order to pick them except perhaps in very special circumstances.

But now consider a problem that may arise even for the ethical codes of respectable occupations, such as computing and librarianship. If such codes make certain demands, how do we satisfy both these demands and those more generally applicable to humankind? Is it just a matter of doing what is appropriate in our own field, as well as observing universal principles such as "Do no murder"? Unfortunately it is not as simple as this, because sometimes there may be a conflict between a general ethic and an acknowledged professional one; it may be very much in the public interest but professionally unethical for a priest to tell the police what he has heard in the confessional box, whereas if I or the priest were to overhear the same thing in a bar we should tell them. Maybe our professional ethics should not always override our general ones, but sometimes, it is thought, they should. In early 1996 the Australian Medical Association (AMA) issued a new code of ethics saying that doctors should "keep in confidence information . . . and divulge it only with the patient's permission. Exceptions may arise where the health of others is at risk or you are required by order of a court to breach patient confidentiality." The example of HIV infection comes readily to mind, and concern has been expressed by representatives of high-risk groups that the

AMA is threatening to "overturn the fundamental principles of confidentiality" (*Sunday Age* 7/1/96: 6).

Be this as it may, where do the various codes stand on the issue of possible conflict between general ethical principles and those of professional ethics? The preamble to the ACM Code of Ethics says this:

> It is understood that some words and phrases in a code of ethics are subject to varying interpretations, and that any ethical principle may conflict with other ethical principles in specific situations. Questions related to ethical conflicts can best be answered by thoughtful consideration of fundamental principles, rather than reliance on detailed regulations. (ACM 1992)

While this does not explicitly mention conflict between professional and general ethics, it does leave open that possibility. The ACS is slightly more specific:

> The ACS accepts that the standards are ideal, and may not all be achievable at all times in all circumstances. In practice, a member may occasionally find that some standards conflict with other standards, *including standards from other sources*. On these occasions the member must weigh up the relevant factors and choose to act in the manner which is most consistent with the Code of Ethics, given the circumstances. [Our emphasis] (ACS 1993: section "Standard of Conduct")

The position is complicated, however, by the fact that the ACM Code says that a member should "contribute to society and human well-being" (1.1). This is expanded in the guidelines thus: "This principle concerning the quality of life of all people affirms an obligation to protect fundamental human rights. . . . An essential aim of computing professionals is to minimize negative consequences of computing systems, including threats to health and safety." In a similar manner, the ACS Code says that a member should resolve to "serve the interests of my clients and employers, my employees and students, and the community generally, as matters of no less priority than the interests of myself or my colleagues" (Section 1).

Do these statements allow the member to do what the priest is not supposed to do, and divulge confidential information for the public good? Whatever the codes may mean, such issues will be addressed in various chapters of this book.

THE RESTRICTED SENSE OF "PROFESSION"

Those who speak of professional people and professional ethics often have in mind a more restricted sense than the one above. Not just any occupation will count. Professions are distinguished from, and often seen as superior to, trades and other occupations: Pocket picking and prostitution may be professions in the broad sense, with the latter indeed the oldest of them all, but they are definitely not professions in the restricted sense, neither of them being, in the words of the *Shorter Oxford Dictionary*, "a vocation in which a professed knowledge of some department of learning is used in its application to the affairs of others, or in the practice of an art founded upon it." The notion was originally applied specifically to the three "learned" professions of divinity, law, and medicine, and later to the military one; the category of people commonly called professionals (in the restricted and privileged sense) is now larger and includes engineers of various sorts, teachers, researchers, bankers, accountants, politicians, and so on. Many computer people, including engineers, software developers, consultants, and network administrators, would be regarded as covered as well, and so would many librarians and others in the information field. Is this appropriate?

The restricted concept of a profession is helpfully developed in a recent article by Robert Fullinwider. Professionals, he says, are persons whose special role is defined by (1) an orientation to public good, (2) a specialised knowledge and training, and (3) a dependent, vulnerable clientele (Fullinwider 1995: 2). These criteria seem to be satisfied fairly well by all the candidates in the first two groups above, especially if we interpret the first criterion generously; we could say at any rate that some of them are at least supposed to serve the public good, and in particular the needs of their dependent and vulnerable clienteles, and that this is enough to count. Many people in the computer world serve the needs of clients who are dependent on their specialised knowledge; should they be classified as professionals too? And, because they have such clients, they surely have a moral responsibility to use their knowledge with care and due respect for those clients' needs, as well as to those of the computer world at large: They are subject, that is to say, to the relevant demands of professional ethics.

This is all very well. But people in many other occupations—ones not generally called professions—have dependent and vulnerable clients too. Train drivers, electricians, plumbers, and others have knowledge and training that the rest of us do not have, and we are very much in their hands. Accordingly, the electrician wiring our house has a moral obligation to do it safely, over and above the general obligations he or she has to refrain from stealing our property, to summon help as appropriate in an emergency, and so on. So why are such people not called professionals, in the restricted as well as the broad sense?

One answer might be that while many such people certainly do have such clients, and use special knowledge and training in serving their needs, academic learning is also essential to membership of a profession in the restricted sense. How much is there in this? Historically, the differences between say lawyers and doctors on the one hand and tradespeople on the other may have been greater than they are now; lawyers and doctors not only attended universities but also learned Latin, whereas thatchers and cobblers may have been hardly able to read and write. Nowadays the Latin has gone and virtually everyone is literate in his or her native language. Further, the actual work of the lawyer or doctor consists largely of exercising skills—guidance of a client in the best direction, or advocacy in the courtroom—and many technical college courses involve theoretical studies. Nevertheless, let us concede that there remains a significant difference in academic emphasis between the training and work of the professional people on one hand and the nonprofessionals on the other. Yet it is hard to see how such a difference could be very relevant, in itself, to the issue of professional ethics. Could the mere fact that X is more academically learned than Y be a basis for saying that X has more duties, or more stringent duties, toward her vulnerable clients than Y has toward his? It may be that a certain level of mental development is required for one to have any moral duties at all, but we are thinking here of groups of people far above that threshold, wherever it may lie. Many people who are said to practise a trade, rather than a profession, have plenty of intelligence and indeed plenty of learning in their chosen fields.

Nevertheless, the fact remains that, even if partly for historical reasons that are not so clearly valid today, many members of professions (in the restricted sense) enjoy a higher social status, and an accordingly higher income, than many other folk. High social status is certainly not exclusive to such people—sports stars often enjoy it, though it depends very much on the particular sport and the particular society. People such as the beautiful, the rulers and their relatives and friends, and those seen as gifted with medical or mystic powers, may enjoy it too. But, though high status is not exclusive to professionals, here we do have something that is relevant to the matter of moral responsibilities. For when a person does enjoy such status, for whatever reason and however good it is, it seems that we are entitled to expect a high standard of conduct and to be comparatively intolerant of delinquency. In some cases we may have such an attitude because we believe that the person has not earned his or her high status, but has acquired it by being, for example, a member of a royal family without having the responsibilities of actual sovereignty. Or perhaps we may be thinking of the trust that many ordinary folk place in those of high status—maybe not so much in the beautiful or the athletically gifted, but often in princes and priests and prophets—and of the wrongness of betraying that trust in various ways. A third consideration, applying generally to those of high status, is their power to set examples, both good and bad, to their many admirers—who may, especially perhaps those of sportspeople and pop stars, be quite young and impressionable. With this point in mind many people were disappointed, to put it mildly, when a very high-profile football star was discharged without a conviction recently after admitting to a crude sexual assault on a woman in a city street. It is sometimes said in defence of such people that they are under great stress because of their celebrity status. Stress there may well be, but it is hard to see how it comes anywhere near providing an excuse for behaviour that harms, threatens, or upsets others.

People who have an occupation recognised as a profession tend to have a comparatively high social status—maybe not as high as many of them would like, or as high as that of pop stars and footballers, but high nevertheless. And, even if every professional person has earned that status, the second and third points above would appear to be applicable to most of them—people place trust in them, often because they see no alternative, and they are well placed to set influential examples to others. Consequently, professionals (like others of high status) have particularly solid obligations to do the right thing. It may be noted that at least one of the traditional professions, divinity, does not, at least in modern Western society, enjoy the status it once did and still does in some mainly conservative places. In this case, however, the points about trust and example are highly applicable because of the particular nature of this profession, at least in its ministering dimension as distinct from, say, its academic one. Many people place great and intimate trust in their clergy and rely on them for moral as well as spiritual guidance, which makes it more shocking when a priest sexually abuses a young or vulnerable person in his care than when a clothing shop manager does the same thing to a customer in a changing room. To say this is not, of course, to defend the manager.

What about computer and information people? Do they enjoy a high enough social status to make a difference to their moral responsibilities to their dependent clients or to society in general? It may depend very much on the nature of one's work—whether one is a top IBM executive or a humble programmer in a government department—and also on the social group in question: In some social circles, anyone who can even operate a computer is revered. But should they have such a status? And—though this is not the same question—should they be classed as members of a profession in the restricted sense?

The case for librarians, for example, is well argued by Roberts and Konn (1990). They observe that although some decades ago sociologists were apt to dismiss librarianship as a nonprofession because of doubts about its knowledge base, it does in fact qualify clearly on this score. Its specialised knowledge base encompasses three main parts. First, there is a body of management principles, derived partly from sources external to librarianship and of more general application, but adapted and reviewed continually by way of research and formal courses. Second, modern librarians need to have wide-ranging technical expertise, contrary to a popular impression of them as "little more than clerks concerned with recording the movement of books in and out of their libraries, or as rather superior warehouse keepers" (Roberts and Konn 1990: 100). Many of these fields of course now involve applications of computer systems, and librarians have been prominent in developing the sophistication and usefulness of those applications. The third area of their expertise is what Roberts and Konn call "contextual": There is "a fund of abstract and practical knowledge which interacts with management and technical knowledge to provide professional vision and the maintenance of professional standards" (103). Like the other two, it is formed and refreshed in a variety of ways including formal study, discussion, and experience, and in the case of academic libraries, for example, it includes such disparate elements as knowledge of the institutional power structure, of the needs and demands of particular user groups and individuals, of other libraries, of friendly and unfriendly forces and factions, and of relevant trends at home and abroad. Such strands of knowledge assist in the making of "fine judgements of consequences and skilled choices of alternatives. Such choices are the essence of professionality" (Roberts and Konn 1990: 105).

Without disputing any such claims as to the demands and potential of the work, we have some ambivalence, however, as to whether librarianship and comparable occupations in computing and information ought to be counted as professions. On the one hand, there is the legitimate concern on the part of advocates such as Roberts and Konn, and many library associations, that the skills and responsibilities are apt to be underrated by those in high places who make policy and budgetary decisions. Workloads that compromise such skills and responsibilities are imposed, or positions are downgraded and work that ought to be done by knowledgeable, highly skilled people is seen as suitable for people much less so. In such circumstances it is easy to have a sense not only of increased personal difficulty or insecurity, but also of an affront to one's professional standing.

On the other hand, we have a concern that has nothing to do with librarians or computer people in particular, or with appropriate recognition in the workplace and its administration of the nature and importance of such jobs. Rather, it is a concern about society at large and the according of high or not-so-high status to someone on the basis of whether he or she is seen to be a professional. We favour a society of a comparatively egalitarian temper, a society in which there is not a pronounced scale in terms of status but in which everybody, or at least everybody leading a worthwhile life, is given recognition and respect. The category of people leading worthwhile lives is intended to be very broad and to include not only doctors and lawyers and teachers, but also folk of many other sorts including computer and information people, business people, tradespeople, homemakers, cleaners, artists, clerics, and even politicians. This is not to say that everyone in each of these categories leads a worthwhile life—some in each deliberately do mischief, and some a lot of it. Nor is it to say that only people who lead worthwhile lives deserve respect. There are some who are too aged, too sick, or too disabled to lead a life that could really be regarded as worthwhile in any significant way, but who should still be accorded respect, though the appropriate type will differ from that due to those whose lives are sensitive to social interaction in a richer variety of ways. The way you should behave toward your frail and senile 95-year-old grandmother is obviously different from the way you should treat a junior colleague at work or a person you employ to work on your house.

Thus we are hesitant to recommend that computer and information people should be classed as professionals rather than nonprofessionals, though this is in no way meant as a slight. It is because the distinction should, in our view, be played down; it is unfortunate if it needs to be invoked to protect people from improper pressures or threats of the kind mentioned above. In a social context we should not seek to evaluate a worker according to whether he or she is a member of a profession, and in an employment context we should focus on the nature of the job itself (whatever it might be) and on the conditions required for it to be done effectively, with all relevant criteria considered and in an appropriate order of priority.

There is, however, a similar-looking but very different question that we may well ask about a worker. This is the question of whether he or she has what is often called a "professional attitude," whatever the job might be. Such an attitude will involve taking pride in one's work, trying to do it as well as possible, and actively considering ways in which it might be done better, taking all relevant considerations into account. Admittedly, there is more scope for the exercise of such an attitude in some fields of employment than in others: A repetition worker on a factory production line (and it may be a factory making computer parts) may not have much scope for reflection on how she might do her job better or for pride in doing it well. But in a great many types of work, both professional and nonprofessional in traditional terms, and certainly including many types of work with computers and information, there is ample scope for a professional attitude, and such an attitude should be encouraged and appreciated.

What are the consequences of this discussion for professional ethics? In some sense there are no professional ethics as this is often understood. But there is something like an occupational ethic. The practitioners of many different occupations have responsibilities to others over and above the responsibilities that they have as human beings. An electrician has special responsibilities with respect to the wiring of houses, just as a medical

---------------------- **3** ----------------------

Freedom, Information, and Images

To coerce a man is to deprive him of freedom—freedom from what? Almost every moralist in human history has praised freedom. Like happiness and goodness, like nature and reality, the meaning of this term is so porous that there is little interpretation that it seems able to resist. (Berlin 1969: 121)

Many of the ethical questions about information concern freedom at some level. Some of these freedoms include freedom of expression, of opinion, of speech, of information, freedom to copy, to own and to read, and freedom from interference and observation. Some of these freedoms clash with others, and some are best discussed under different headings. The last, for example, is really a matter of privacy, and will be discussed in a chapter of its own. The freedoms to copy and to own are issues in intellectual property, and will also have a chapter to themselves. We are left then with the freedoms of expression, opinion, speech and information, and the freedom to read. These are all in some way related to censorship, and all except freedom of information will be discussed in our examination of censorship in the next chapter. Freedom of information is best considered on its own because not only does it have little to do with freedom of expression and opinion, but it also raises questions of privacy and access in a way not done by the other freedoms. Another freedom related to computer technology and to information in general is the freedom to manipulate images. This is less often discussed, but is of growing importance. This chapter will focus on freedom of information and freedom to manipulate images.

Because the notion of freedom is frequently mentioned but seldom examined, this chapter begins with a brief general discussion of this concept,
concentrating particularly on J. S. Mill's famous argument for liberty that
is based on a distinction between *self-regarding* and *other-regarding* actions,
that is, between actions affecting nobody except oneself, and those affecting others (1859). We first apply this to freedom of information and then
to the relatively new field of digital image manipulation. The former asks
questions about what people should be allowed to know, and the latter
about what they should be free to do to and with digital images. Of particular interest are the roles played by lying and deception, and the production of pornography by image manipulation.

FREEDOM

A lot of nonsense is spoken about freedom. We often speak as if it is
some kind of absolute good, as if the most important thing in the world is
to be free. But it is not clear what this means, and it is almost certain that
it is not true anyway. There are lots of "goods" in this world, and while
freedom, spelled out properly, is undoubtedly one of them, and perhaps
even the most valuable, it is only one. My freedom may clash with the
well-being of others, with the good of society as a whole, and even with
my own good. The best way to look at freedom is to consider it with respect to particular aspects of life. We should look at the freedom to do certain things and to live in various ways, and at freedom from certain
restrictions. What do I want to be free from? What do I want to be free to
do? What should I be free from and free to do? Should I have the freedom
to say and read anything or to manipulate and use images in any way, or
should there be some restrictions, and if there should be, what should
they be and how can they be justified?

Before looking more closely at the specific questions of image manipulation and censorship, we will briefly see what Mill had to say on freedom in general. We can then look at those areas in the light of his theory.
Mill begins with an examination of "the nature and limits of the power
which can be legitimately exercised by society over the individual" (1859:
3). We must establish the right principles for deciding on the restrictions
that should be placed on individual freedom. Some restrictions are
clearly required if we are to live happily in a society, simply because there
is frequently a clash of interests between different individuals, and between the interests of the state as a whole and the interests of particular
individuals in the state. According to Mill, there is just one principle,
which is:

> that the sole end for which mankind are warranted, individ-
> ually or collectively, in interfering with the liberty of action of

any of their number, is self-protection. That the only purpose for which power can be rightfully exercised over any member of a civilised community, against his will, is to prevent harm to others. His own good, either physical or moral, is not a sufficient warrant. (1859: 10–11)

So there is justification in limiting someone's freedom to do something only if what they want to do will harm someone else. There is no justification, he believes, in stopping people from doing things that will harm only themselves. This is emphasised again: "Over himself, over his own body and mind, the individual is sovereign" (Mill 1859: 11). Mill qualifies this principle in several ways. First he stresses that this principle is meant to apply only to people "in the maturity of their faculties." Children, and those who are obviously ignorant or irrational, may be legitimately subjected to paternalism, that is, coerced to save them from harm. The second qualification concerns that which affects only the individual. Mill realises that many, perhaps most actions affect more than one person, and therefore it is not so easy to identify those actions that will harm only oneself. So there may be few or no nontrivial actions affecting only one person, robbing his dictum of most of its force. If I live alone, how I arrange my furniture may not affect others at all, providing that I have no visitors. But this is pretty trivial and of little moral importance. To try to overcome this problem Mill says that individuals should be free to do as they like with respect to actions affecting only themselves "directly and in the first instance" (1859: 13) or primarily affecting only themselves. There are difficulties in interpreting some of these concepts, and it is not clear that Mill himself remains entirely faithful to his principles throughout the essay, but his "harm to others" principle is a good reference point.

How does Mill justify this view of liberty? He was a utilitarian (a theory we first met in chapter 1); that is, he believed that the morally right action was that which produced more happiness than any viable alternative action:

> The creed which accepts as the foundation of morals, "utility" or the "greatest happiness principle" holds that actions are right in proportion as they tend to promote happiness; wrong as they tend to produce the reverse of happiness. By happiness is intended pleasure, and the absence of pain; by unhappiness, pain, and the privation of pleasure. (Mill 1863: 11)

Allowing individuals freedom in those areas in which nobody else is harmed is the best way to promote happiness. In general, I am more likely to be happy if I can do more or less as I like than if someone else controls what I do. According to Mill, in normal cases the individual is a better judge of what is best for him or her than is someone else. So in order to promote happiness, the individual should have as much liberty as is compatible with others having an equal amount.

FREEDOM AND INFORMATION

When people speak of freedom *of* information, they are usually referring to those acts passed by many governments that give citizens the right of access to government documents. An important aspect of this is the right to information about themselves. This must be distinguished from the *accessibility* of information, which refers to all information (except that legitimately protected by privacy, etc). The latter is what the American Library Association has in mind in its report *Freedom and Equality of Access to Information*, which states:

> Knowledge is power. We have known that from the beginning. How freely and how equally citizens have access to knowledge determines how freely and how equally they can share in the governing of our society and in the work and rewards of our economy. (ALA 1986: 1)

As important as both freedom of information and access to information are, these are general issues and not of immediate concern here. Our concern is with problems that are raised in new or more urgent ways by the new information processing machines, that is, computers. So what freedom of information issues, if any, are raised in a unique way (or raised for the first time) by computer technology? There seem to be two: personal data stored in databases, and access to information on the Internet. The first, personal information, has various aspects: (1) the information actually stored, (2) information about the *type* of information stored, (3) who collects it and stores it, (4) the purpose for which it is collected and stored, (5) who has access to it. The second, freedom and access to information on the Internet, also has a number of aspects, but these have more to do with the *freedom* than with the *information*. It is not only *information* that has more than one meaning. *Freedom* is also ambiguous. In this context it has two distinct and equally important aspects: one is as a right, the other an ability. I am free in the fullest sense to access information if (a) I have the legal right to do so, (b) I have the ability to do so; that is, I have the skill (or someone with the skill to help me), (c) I can afford to do it, and (d) the relevant facilities are located where I have access to them. If these latter conditions are not satisfied, the legal right amounts to little.

Personal Information

This is discussed again later with respect to privacy. Here the emphasis is on the individual's right to access information about himself or herself, given that it is stored. There are several reasons why there ought to be this access. One is that it is about the individual. The burden of proof is on those wishing to stop him or her having that access. Another reason is the utilitarian one concerning the accuracy of the information. Correct information about me can be used against me, but the dangers of incorrect information being so used are much greater. But there is more to it than this. The individual requires access to information about the type of information stored, who collects and stores it and why, and who else has access to it. This is freedom of access to *meta*-information. Without this freedom there may be no awareness that there is information to which freedom of access is required. There may be legal or moral rights to information access, but if we do not know about the information and its importance, these rights are of little value.

If individuals should be free in all areas in which nobody else is harmed, then freedom of personal information would seem to be one of the more obvious freedoms, at least concerning that information collected and stored by the government. The exceptions might be data required for security reasons or criminal investigations. Here it might be in the interests of the vast majority that someone does not know what is known about them. What is the situation where the information is collected and stored by private companies or businesses? Now ownership of databases becomes an issue. If some business invests time and money into the creation of a database of personal information, does it also have a right to restrict access to it by those about whom information is stored? Aspects of this issue are also discussed later, but here the important one is the individual's right to see, and, if necessary, have changed, the information in a privately owned database. Given the potential for harm to the individual if this freedom is restricted and the lack of harm likely to result from this freedom, it would again seem obvious that it is something we ought to have. Freedom of personal information here should override some of the rights typically connected to private property. My ownership of a database containing information about you does not give me the moral right to stop you from having access to the information about yourself. (It is not even clear that I own it, but that will arise again in the later discussion of intellectual property.)

The importance of freedom of meta-information was mentioned in connection with government information. It is no less important for privately held information. In fact, to give some bite to the freedom of information, the meta-information should be made public and not just be available to the public. Governments and others who hold personal information have a moral obligation to publicise what type of information they hold. Otherwise freedom of information largely comes to nought.

Internet Access

Freedom to access information on the Internet involves both the *right* to access it, and the *ability*. The issue of rights is closely related to censorship and will be considered in the next chapter. Here the focus will be on ability and the closely related question of equality of access.

There are at least three factors that are relevant to someone's ability to access the information on the Internet: skill, location, and wealth.

Skill. Illiteracy has always created a problem in access to information, at least since the written word has been paramount for its storage and dissemination. The illiterate obviously cannot read newspapers, books, or the print on computer screens. But the problem moves to another level with Internet information. Even literate people might lack the computer skills necessary to access this information. It might be that anyone who can learn to read can learn to use a computer. But that is not obviously true because they are different skills and may not always be transferable.

Location. In some countries this may not pose a problem, but in others it does. Access to the Internet involves communication channels, most commonly telephone lines. In geographically large countries like Australia with areas remote from centres of population, communications in these remote areas are often poorer and much more expensive than in the large centres and between them. Those living in remote areas have always been "information poor" in the sense that library resources have been scarce or nonexistent, with newspapers days or weeks late, and so on. The Internet has the potential to overcome this, but only if telephone services in those areas are of a comparable standard and price with those in more densely settled areas. If they are not, the "information poor" will become even poorer relative to the "information rich" who will have easy access to all of the information available on the Internet.

Wealth. Libraries are mostly free and newspapers cost only a little, but computers are still relatively expensive. While those on low incomes have always had less access to information than those on high incomes, they have always been able, if literate and not in remote areas, to get information from libraries and newspapers. Access to the Internet is much more difficult. Unless one can afford the relevant computing equipment or has access to it through the workplace, normally one has no way of reaching this information, and most of those with access at work are not among the poor. Those on low incomes are likely to become even more information poor.

What has emerged from this discussion of freedom of access to information on the Internet is that *equality* is just as important as freedom.

Equality of access gives some teeth to freedom of information. Equality in itself of course is not very important. Just stop everyone from having access and we have equality. What makes it important is that if there is the right to freedom of access to this information, then some people (the wealthy, etc.) can exercise that right. In this situation, the actual one, an emphasis on equality will help the less well off also exercise their right. A concentration only on freedom in this context places too much emphasis on rights and not enough on abilities.

The Importance of Freedom of Information

It has already been suggested that the freedom of personal information is vital for utilitarian reasons; it helps safeguard the individual's rights. It can also be argued that because such freedom harms nobody, except in certain circumstances, nobody has the right to curtail it. Another argument might be that we just have a right, perhaps a "natural right," to access any information about ourselves.

What are the arguments for freedom and equality of access to Internet information? Again there is the one based on Mill's "harm to others" principle. If it causes no harm to others, access should be allowed. There is also the utilitarian argument that individuals are better off the more information that they have. "Knowledge is power," it is said. This argument also supports the equality of access. It is also commonly argued that wide access to information is essential for democracy. There would seem to be some truth in this. A more informed society should be able to make better decisions.

These arguments generally support both freedom and equality, but equality can be argued for independently. Some level of equality of information access would just seem to be fair. Why we should try to be fair is another matter, but it does seem a little odd even to raise this question.

Obligations of Information Professions and Professionals

It is one thing to say that people should have the freedoms discussed above. It is another to say what role, if any, information professionals and their professional bodies have in ensuring that these freedoms can be exercised. As information professionals, they clearly have an obligation to assist in the gathering of information (within limits discussed in chapter 8). This is particularly true in the case of those unskilled in the use of the new information technology. There is also some plausibility in the view that information professionals and their professional organisations should work toward greater Internet access for the general population. Internet access in libraries is one possibility and so-called "Internet cafes" another. Without this, freedom of access to information amounts to little, as we have already seen. It may be, of course, that if the Internet were used by most of the population it would become almost useless because of the volume of traffic. That may be, but some equitable way of distributing access still needs to be found, providing another challenge for the information professional.

FREEDOM AND IMAGE MANIPULATION

The manipulability of images by means of modern digital technology also raises various ethical concerns to do with freedom. What should individuals be free to do with images? How might one person's freedom here impinge on the rights of others, and in which cases does it matter? The issues are not essentially new, but they are given new urgency by the ease and undetectability that the new technology affords. The essence of this new technology is the digital storage of images. These images can be created by cameras, by scanning hard copies, or by operating the computer itself. Once they are stored digitally, they can be copied as easily as any other file. In a few minutes I could copy an image and pass it off as my own work, with the copy being in no way inferior to the original. (In fact it is unclear that the old distinction between copy and original holds here. This will be considered in the next chapter.) And changes can be made without leaving any trace of the alterations. Electronic changes are scientifically undetectable (Duguid 1994: 6). Using techniques like "tweening" (creating frames, that is, images, which are between other frames), "warping" (stretching and shrinking images or parts of images), and "morphing" (changing one image into another) (Anderson 1993), as well as the more familiar cutting and pasting, images can be juxtapositioned, and shapes, textures, and colours can be altered in all sorts of ways. William Mitchell describes it like this:

> Such fake "photographs" can now be produced by using widely available "paint" and image-processing software to rearrange, recolor and otherwise transform the elements of a scene. The same software can combine fragments of different images into one new image. Other software can generate completely synthetic photorealistic pictures by applying sophisticated perspective projection and shading to digital models of three-dimensional scenes. (1994: 45)

There is nothing new in the ability to copy, manipulate, and enhance photographs and other images, apart from the technology. "Trick photography" has been around for decades, but what was once possible only with considerable time and skill is now becoming commonplace. And of central importance, as previously noted, is that these manipulations leave no traces. There is no cutting of film or paper or altering of lines on any sort of hard copy. And copying does not degrade the original. Our concern now is with the uses made of these manipulated images (in the next chapter we will look at the manipulation of digital images with respect to ownership). The issues are whether there is any manipulating that should not be done, or any uses to which these images should not be put. Or should there be complete freedom?

The Ethics of Manipulating Images

The ethical questions to be discussed here concern the uses to which manipulated images might be put. A central worry here is that publishing or distributing an image that we know to have been manipulated amounts to a form of lying. Standardly, lying consists in making a verbal statement we know to be false, with the intention to deceive; but may we not do essentially the same thing with a picture? Not every alteration or manipulation of an image, of course, is so intended. We may be correcting a technical flaw in the photograph, or even trying to make a colour more faithful to that of the photographed object—to avoid the viewer being deceived into thinking that its colour is other than it really is. But obviously an image may also be manipulated with the intention of deceiving. To take a now celebrated example, a magazine cover photograph during the 1991 Gulf War showed U.S. President George Bush with Jordan's King Hussein, when in fact they had never met; the picture had been composed from separate originals. One may well regard it as effectively stating that they were together, and believe that it was published with the intention of deceiving people into thinking not only that they had met but, more importantly, that Jordan sympathised with the United States in its conflict with Iraq.

Is it always wrong to lie? The great and famously uncompromising moral philosopher Immanuel Kant (Rachels 1986: 109) thought so. He held that even if some innocent person is hiding from a potential murderer who comes along and asks you where he is and you believe that telling the truth will result in murder, you ought to tell the truth. Nearly everyone else would say that, particularly if you are in no danger yourself, you not only may tell a lie but ought to. An innocent person's life is simply far more important than telling the truth. Yet while we may not accept Kant's absolute prohibition on lying, many of us see it as a very serious business—so much so that even in the case of the would-be murderer we may feel very strongly inclined to try to protect the potential victim while not telling a lie. We may refuse to answer the question or evade it; we may, as someone once suggested, answer honestly but bar his way; or we may speak the truth but misleadingly so, by saying, for example, "I saw him at the end of the street five minutes ago," not mentioning that we helped him to hide in this very house only one minute ago. Such strategies have obvious drawbacks. The first may well expose us to greater danger, or give the hunter a pretty good idea of the location of his quarry, or both; the second depends on our ability to bar him safely and effectively; and the third may expose us to further questioning, to which it may be difficult to give true but misleading answers. Kant, incidentally, did not show any interest in any of these possibilities; he simply thought that one should answer the would-be murderer honestly. Yet the fact that such "solutions" are to many of us so appealing bears witness to our reluctance to tell a straight-out lie, even in such a case as this.

Now if we see image manipulation as a form of lying, at least where it is done with the intent to deceive, should we take it very seriously? There are several possible responses to this question. One is to play down the matter by resisting the idea that it is a form of lying. There is, after all, no verbal statement, and thus no verbal statement that is false or believed to be false. And is this not an essential element in lying? Maybe it is, but maybe what is really objectionable in lying is the intention to deceive; we do not object to people making false statements in telling jokes, or when acting in plays or reciting poems, because there is here no such intention. And so when there is such an intention in the manipulation of images, whether or not we use the word "lying," is it not just as morally objectionable? (A corollary of this argument is that the common desire to make a true but misleading statement rather than a false and misleading one is misguided—a true but intentionally misleading one is in the same moral boat as a lie.)

Another response to the assimilation of image manipulation to lying is to suggest that lying is not as bad as all that. It is not only allowable, or indeed obligatory, to lie in such a case as that of Kant's murderer; it is allowable to lie in order to save others and even oneself from various lesser evils. Suppose a man with some power or authority over a woman in their workplace asks her a very intrusive question about her personal life. Even if he is not her official superior he may be an exploitative and manipulative person, and she may have good reason to expect that neither refusing to answer nor evading the question will be in her best interest and may in any case give him a pretty fair idea of the truth. In such a case, would it be wrong of her to lie to him? If the circumstances permit, it may be wiser for her to refuse to answer and then complain about his intrusion or harassment, but the circumstances may not be like that. We may perhaps be concerned that, if she can tell him a convincing lie, then maybe she has become practised by lying in less legitimate cases; we may also be worried that even if this is not so, she may be setting foot on a "slippery slope" leading her to lie for less and less legitimate reasons. Both of these concerns should be heeded, but neither of them shows that her lying in this case—to protect a legitimate interest of hers—would be wrong. It should be seen as no more immoral than wearing makeup to conceal a skin blemish or digitally removing such a blemish from a photograph of oneself, both of which are (in normal circumstances) legitimate cases of deception.

Yet obviously many lies are morally indefensible, and many of the deceptions facilitated by image manipulation may be morally suspect too. A practitioner in the manipulation field, Dale Duguid, expresses his concern at the counterfeiting capacities that have progressed from the audiotape to the still photograph to video imagery to motion pictures of high degrees of resolution:

> Rapid technological change has always caused harm to some, while providing advantages for others. Those implementing the new technology are usually the advantaged. Rapid technological change causes everything from species and culture extinctions to displacement and dysfunction in our societies. No change has been more rapid, and has greater potential to create [social] dysfunction than current advances in image manipulation. What happens when you or the news editor can no longer rely on what he or she sees with his/her eyes in the domain of still or moving pictures of any resolution? (1994: 11)

However, another recent writer, Sean Callahan, suggests that there is not too much cause for concern after all: "The fulminations over the ethics of digital manipulation are partly based on the cliché a picture doesn't lie.' Yet if a truth-in-photography law existed, the Federal Trade Commission would have banned photographs in advertising years ago" (Callahan 1993: 64). He outlines three reasons why there is not much to worry about. First, "Those who argue that editorial photographs represent reality ignore the fact that a camera shutter operating at one-250th of a second can't possibly tell the whole truth about a scene, and that the rectangular frame takes in only a fraction of reality" (Callahan 1993: 64). A photograph *is* only a very small piece of reality. Seen out of context it can be very misleading, particularly when taken together with a caption. Equally misleading can be a photograph intentionally placed in the wrong context. Second, Callahan rightly points out that skilled people could always modify photographs: "The hand that today operates the mouse running Photoshop is essentially the same one that once handled a razor blade and airbrush though the technology democratizes the once tight little world of the highly skilled, highly paid retouchers" (Callahan 1993: 64). All that has changed is the technology and the level of skill required. Third and finally, newspaper and magazine editors are bound to give accurate information or sales will drop off. It is therefore in their own interests not to tamper with photographs in a manner likely to mislead:

> What remains firmly in the hands of the editors . . . is a franchise based on accurate information. As soon as their customers

start getting misleading information, that franchise starts to wither. Despite the fears of many photographers, common sense suggests that the same ethical standards editors apply to the other facets of the news-gathering process will prevail in the photography department. (Callahan 1993: 64)

While all of Callahan's points are true to some extent, they are not much cause for comfort. "A picture doesn't lie" has always been a dubious claim, but with image manipulation techniques and current software, the scope for "lying" has been greatly expanded. Much greater changes to photographs and other images are now possible much more quickly and cheaply, and in much greater number. If the software is available, no high level of skill is required and no traces of the manipulation remain. This takes care of his first two points. The third point is at best true for current or recent news, but not for historical records. Archival images are not subject to the public's accuracy requirements in the way that newspapers might be. But there are also problems for current and recent news. Remoteness in space lessens the public's control over the accuracy of reports just as remoteness in time does. In short, the case has not been made that ethical issues are not raised in new and more urgent ways.

Manipulating and Entertaining

So far we have focussed on political uses of image manipulation, but it may also be used for entertainment—which of course may also mean for the sake of the money to be had in the entertainment industry. This may seem innocuous, and no doubt it often is, but several concerns may arise. For one thing, as Duguid points out, the line between entertainment and history may not always be correctly located: "Actual archival footage can be reprocessed through image synthesis ostensibly for entertainment purposes and then returned to the archival domain—its subtle changes forever becoming part of documented history and collective memory" (1994: 13).

Secondly, what is done for the sake of entertainment may have directly political aspects as well. Duguid refers to a film about World War I, based on original black and white footage, with real 1990s actors among real 1916 troops on the Somme, all in living colour—yet the mud is shown as grey, not as the purple it would actually have been in that bloodbath. This has the effect of "sanitising the new interpretation" (Duguid 1994: 10). Such a thing might be done for the political motive of controlling viewers' impressions of the horrors of war; more probably in the present case it was done to prevent the film being too sickening to be maximally entertaining and profitable, but with the possible consequence nevertheless that some viewers' impressions are a little less horrific than they would otherwise have been. On the other hand, for many viewers there are no such constraints on entertainment; the gorier and more violent the scene the more exciting and enjoyable it is. And digital image manipulation allows ample scope for the gratification of such tastes. Beheadings and impalings and other such delights may be made as explicit as desired; no longer need an unsuspecting actor die as in a "snuff movie," though there is still the fact that for some viewers there is apparently pleasure not only in seeing lethal violence but in knowing that the person filmed has actually suffered it.

This leads us to pornography, a topic to which we will return in the discussions of both censorship and virtual reality. Some pornography is violent and some is not, and image manipulation may be used in both. Many hold that pornography is harmful in that it is a factor in causing sexual assaults and promoting sexually exploitative attitudes in men toward women; others hold that it is harmless, or should at least be regarded as innocent until proven guilty, and still others hold that it actually does good in serving as a "safety valve," giving satisfaction to some people who would otherwise have raped or molested, quite apart from the pleasure enjoyed by the consumer. Some see the distinction between violent and nonviolent pornography as very important and argue that the former is worse, or the only bad kind, because it is more harmful and/or objectionable in itself. The arguments here are complex. Does the advent of digital image manipulation affect them substantially? It is not clear that it does, although it may allow interesting variations in equipment and performance—variations that are likely to be exaggerations and may create unrealistic impressions and expectations in the innocent. More seriously, there is also the possibility of respectable photographs of respectable people being rendered pornographic. The harm, if any, caused to those who see such pictures and to those whom they then assault or exploit may be no greater than that done by more conventionally produced pornography. But there is also the possibility of harm to the subject or subjects of the original photograph—to their reputations—due to the general public's disapproval of pornography and of those who participate in the production of it. Alternatively, a subject might be harmed merely in a financial way; the subject may have been willing to pose for pornography, but only for a large fee, of which he or she is being cheated when respectable pictures are made pornographic without his or her knowledge.

How Should We Respond?

Harms of these various kinds, and the risks of them, give grounds for moral concern and, in the clearer cases, condemnation. And where modern image manipulation exacerbates these harms or the risks of them, then obviously we should be morally concerned about it and, in the clearer cases, condemn it. But it is important to distinguish the question of when image manipulation is morally unacceptable from questions of what the law or professional bodies or society in general should do about it. The law is concerned, as is morality, with harms of various tangible kinds: It prohibits sexual assault, for example, and fraud. It also prohibits behaviour that creates the risk of various harms—drunken driving, for example. Should it then also ban pornography, with or without manipulated images, if there is even the risk of its causing harm? And what about its capacity to cause *offence*? There are all sorts of difficult issues here, but they are not perhaps much affected by the technology of image manipulation for they are concerned mainly with the possible or likely effects of what the image shows, rather than with how the picture was produced. There is another category of harms, however, which are both legally problematic and very much affected by the new technology. These are the harms which are caused by, or consist in, deception. They are legally problematic because, while there are clear cases where the law steps in—cases such as fraud and perjury—there are many cases in which the harm is indeterminate and uncertain. Who would be harmed, and how, by being deceived by the Bush-Hussein picture? What if it could be argued plausibly that on balance it would be a good thing for as many people as possible to believe that Jordan was backing the United States? But perhaps this is the wrong question to ask. Is deception bad in itself, apart from any harm it may do to people's material well-being or political security? If so, why does the law tend to concern itself only with those categories of deception that do bring such harms? I may tell you a barefaced lie about my qualifications or achievements, but the law will not touch me unless I am doing so in order to, for example, defraud you in some way. But the scope for deception is, as we have seen, greatly enhanced by the new technology. With its practitioners able to manipulate images in physically undetectable ways, and—contra Callahan—to get away with it, what are we to do?

It might be thought that, if the law is uncertain as to how far its proper interest extends here, and has difficulty in policing it anyway, professional codes of ethics should assume responsibility. They should specify that images should be manipulated only when this causes no significant harm or deception. But apart from the problem of clarifying what is meant by "significant" in each case, there is still the problem of the ease of manipulation coupled with its undetectability. Professional codes of ethics may have some value, but is it realistic to expect them to keep the manipulators sufficiently on the straight and narrow?

It may be that it is not realistic, and that, considering the capacities and temptations of the new technology, we—the consumers of the images— may have to become more wary and less prepared to trust what we see.

When as children we have to learn not to trust people of certain kinds, our innocence suffers a major blow. Will we now have to become less innocent still? If a society is to function at all there must be a considerable level of trust among its members. We know the dangers of trusting too naively the written and spoken word (though most of the time we just have to trust them), but we place great faith in photography, and this has been of great value to us. We can see what is happening in some world trouble spot or in a football match. We can match the spoken word against the picture and make our own judgement about the veracity of the word. But if images may be manipulated at will by political authorities and others with vested interests in deceiving us, a simple test of authenticity is gone.

SUMMARY

We began this chapter by introducing Mill's distinction between *self*-regarding and *other*-regarding actions. His argument is that we ought to have freedom to do as we like in the area of self-regarding actions, that is, those actions that harm, if anybody, only ourselves. Coercion is justified only to prevent harm to others. We then considered what freedoms of information we ought to have, and what we ought to be free to do in the way of manipulating digital images. In general there ought to be freedom to access personal information and information on the Internet, a freedom that involves both rights and abilities. With respect to manipulation, some manipulating does harm others, particularly that which involves lying, inaccurate portrayal of people, and deception. But practical difficulties in preventing such harmful manipulation suggest that we may need to become more sceptical about the veracity of photographs.

REFERENCES

ALA. Commission on Freedom and Equality of Access to Information. 1986. *Freedom and Equality of Access to Information: A Report to the American Library Association*. Chicago: ALA.

Anderson, Scott. 1993. *Morphing Magic*. Indianapolis, IN: Sams Publishing.

Berlin, Isaiah. 1969. *Four Essays on Liberty*. London: Oxford University Press.

Callahan, Sean. 1993. Eye Tech. *Forbes ASAP* 151 (June): 57–67.

Duguid, David. 1994. The morality of synthetic realism. Unpublished paper presented at a conference at Noosa Regional Gallery, Tewantin, Queensland, Australia, March.

Mill, John Stuart. 1859. *On Liberty*; page citations to the edition of David Spitz, 1975.

Mill, John Stuart. 1863. *Utilitarianism*; edition of Sokar Piest, 1957.

Mitchell, William J. 1994. When is seeing believing? *Scientific American* (February): 44–49.

Piest, Sokar, ed. 1957. *John Stuart Mill: Utilitarianism*. New York: Liberal Arts Press.

Rachels, J. 1986. *The Elements of Moral Philosophy*. New York: Random House.

FURTHER READING

Northmore, David. 1990. *Freedom of Information Handbook*. London: Bloomsbury.

Nozick, Robert. 1980. *Anarchy, State, and Utopia*. Oxford: Blackwell.

Rawls, John. 1972. *A Theory of Justice*. Oxford: Oxford University Press.

Ten, C. L. 1980. *Mill on Liberty*. Oxford: Clarendon Press.

4

Censorship of the Internet

Something about the combination of sex and computers, . . . seems to make otherwise worldly-wise adults a little crazy. How else to explain the uproar surrounding the discovery by a U.S. Senator—Nebraska Democrat James Exon—that pornographic pictures can be downloaded from the Internet and displayed on a home computer? This, as any computer-savvy college student can testify, is old news. Yet suddenly the press is on alert, parents and teachers are up in arms, and lawmakers in Washington are rushing to ban the smut from cyberspace with new legislation—sometimes with little regard to either its effectiveness or its constitutionality.

Because of the global nature of the Internet, these images are not limited to the U.S. Some Asian governments are shoring up tough anti-pornography laws to keep the wave of erotica from reaching shores that had been relatively porn-free. Australia's state and federal attorneys-general meet this month to discuss ways of regulating the Internet. Conservative Islamic countries like Saudi Arabia are keeping Internet access tightly controlled. Even the supremely tolerant French are starting to pay attention. (Elmer-Dewitt 1995: 48)

In the previous chapter we considered the notion of freedom and two applications relevant to computing—access to information and digital image manipulation. Censorship, particularly censorship of the Internet, is just another such application, but because of its importance it warrants a chapter in its own right. Here we first try to discover what censorship is and what sorts of arguments can be used to justify it. Giving offence is discussed at some length because of its importance in some justifications of restrictions on freedom of speech. Attention is then turned specifically to censorship of the Internet. We argue that while there might be a *prima facie* case for some censorship, we should consider the value of the Internet as a whole.

WHAT IS CENSORSHIP?

Censorship is a bad thing, or so it is often claimed. Certainly the ALA thinks so. Its *Code of Ethics* states: "We uphold the principles of intellectual freedom and resist all efforts to censor library resources"(II). This might mean that anything in the library collection should be available to all and not subject to any censorship, or it might also mean that in addition to this there should be no censorship applied in the development of the library collection. As we shall see shortly, a position like this leads to some undesirable consequences. But first, what is censorship, and why is it bad? Neither of these questions is as easily answered as is sometimes believed. According to Robert Hauptman, "Censorship is the active suppression of books, journals, newspapers, theater pieces, lectures, discussions, radio and television programs, films, art works, etc.— either partially or in their entirety—that are deemed objectionable on moral, political, military, or other grounds" (1988: 66). A more general definition says that it is "official control over communication" (Giles 1990: 61). While this latter definition does fit the general conception of censorship, it involves some problems. Many of the strongest arguments used against censorship do not work if it is interpreted in this more general way. We will consider these arguments a little later, but first a bit more on what censorship is.

Does all suppression of books and so on constitute censorship? Should, say, a book detailing identifiable people's medical records be published? Almost certainly not, but under the second definition of censorship above, such a restriction would constitute censorship. It could even constitute censorship under Hauptman's definition. It all depends on how "or other grounds" is interpreted. There are two ways to go here. We can look for a definition that excludes cases like this, or we can say that sometimes censorship is justified. Anyone who wants to maintain that censorship is always wrong will have to take the first option (or concede that medical records ought to be allowed to be published!), but it is not clear that this can be done without severe problems. Why do we say that medical records should not be published? Because these records are the business of nobody but the doctor and patient, and to disclose them is an invasion of privacy. Such publishing would be an invasion of privacy, yet prohibiting it fits the definitions of censorship we are considering. So either not all censorship is wrong, or this is not a case of censorship. But if we want to take the second option, how do we rule out the publishing of medical records? We will look at two more examples and then return to this question. Suppose that an advertiser promotes a product with claims that are blatantly false, that is, the advertiser is lying. Is suppression of false advertising censorship? Again it fits the definitions. It is control over communication and it is suppression on moral grounds. And what about the publishing of examination papers before an examination? Perhaps we do not normally think of censorship in connection with these last two examples, but it is not easy to rule them out while leaving in the obvious cases. One possibility would be to append clauses to the definitions, such as, "except where the publishing would be an invasion of privacy" or "except where lies are being told" or "except where the material is an examination," and so on. However, any definition that tried to take account of all cases in which suppression was justifiable would be unworkable. But this is the only possibility if it is to be maintained that all censorship is wrong. A better strategy is to work with a wider definition like Hauptman's, but admit that in some circumstances censorship is justified. We can then examine why some cases are bad and where the lines should be drawn for restrictions on freedom of speech and expression.

Before proceeding further, it is worth mentioning a distinction some may suggest. There is a difference between suppressing a publication because it contains immoral material and suppressing something on the grounds that publishing it is immoral even though there is nothing objectionable about the contents themselves. If we restrict the term "censorship" to the former, then we could say that suppressing pornography, for example, would count as censorship because the material is considered immoral, whereas suppressing the publication of medical records would not count because it is merely to protect privacy. But other examples seem to count against this suggestion. To suppress information because it is politically or militarily sensitive, for instance, is to exercise censorship. And some people favour suppressing pornography not because it is immoral in itself, but to protect people from harm in some way.

In order to raise some other issues about what censorship is, we will see what Article 19 of *The Universal Declaration of Human Rights* says. This will also lead into a discussion of why censorship is thought to be bad. This article states: "Everyone has the right to freedom of opinion and expression; this includes freedom to hold opinions without interference and to seek, receive and impart information and ideas through any media and regardless of frontiers" (*Human Rights Manual* 1993: 140). This implies that censorship in the broad sense of "official control over communication" is a violation of a right. However, when it is examined more closely, it may be seen that several very different things are being claimed under this right. The Article begins by talking of the freedom to hold opinions and freedom of expression. Is this freedom to express opinions, or freedom to express oneself in any way that one wants to? It concludes by saying that this right includes the right "to seek, receive and impart information and ideas." But the right to hold and express an opinion seems to be very different from the right to impart information on how to make bombs or computer viruses.

What is censorship? Even if we accept Hauptman's definition that it is the suppression of books and so on, this question can still be asked at a more general level. Is it restraint on freedom to hold and express opinions, or is it restriction on any communication? We will consider these questions while looking at some of the arguments against censorship. Some of the most compelling come from J. S. Mill (1859). The first argument is that an opinion that is not allowed to be heard just might be true, and the second, that it might contain at least some truth. Therefore, restrictions on the freedom of opinion can, and probably will, deprive the world of some truths. His third reason is that unless beliefs and opinions are vigorously challenged, they will be held as mere prejudices, and finally, those opinions are themselves in danger of dying if never contested, simply because there is never any need to think about them.

The Case against Censorship

Mill's conception of a good human life is one in which we think, reflect, and rationally choose for ourselves among different beliefs and lifestyles according to what seems most true or meaningful to us. This is shown in his arguments for the freedom of expression, to which we now turn. His central tenet here is that people ought to be allowed to express their individuality as they please "so long as it is at their own risk and peril" (Mill 1859: 53). The basic argument is that the diversity created has many benefits. One is that "the human faculties of perception, judgement, discriminative feeling, mental activity, and even moral preference, are exercised only in making a choice" (Mill 1859: 55). And exercising this choice makes it less likely that we will be under the sway of the "despotism of custom" (Mill 1859: 66). We will be able to lead happier and more fulfilled lives. And again, if there is this diversity, each human will be more aware of the various options available, and so more competent to make informed choices in lifestyle and self-expression.

This and other such arguments for freedom of expression do support the claims for lack of restrictions and control of material on the Internet, that is, they support the case against censorship. However, the support is qualified, because one person's right to freedom of expression can impinge on another's rights and can clash with other "goods." There is little sense in the idea of complete freedom of expression for all. So the issue now becomes one of where to draw the line for this freedom. A common criterion is harm to others, which we have met before and which was endorsed by Mill, and another is the giving of offence, in which he was not so interested.

Before considering harm and offence in more detail, we will briefly turn to the freedom to say anything. This can be looked on as being involved in the freedom of expression, but it is useful to mention it separately. In fact, the freedom to say anything at all is not regarded very highly in society. There are all sorts of restrictions on what can be said, and in general there is little opposition to this. There are libel and defamation laws and laws against perjury, blasphemy, abusive language, and so on. There is debate about what should and should not be allowed, but little argument that anything and everything ought to be. The value in having some restrictions on what may be said seems just too obvious. Mill also recognised this and claimed that if certain utterances are likely to cause riots for example, there ought to be restrictions placed on them (1859: 53). So we will return now to the freedom of expression and the notions of harm and offence.

The freedom of expression of one person can cause harm or offence or both to another, so some restrictions need to be placed on how and to what extent a person can be allowed free expression. That there should normally be some restrictions placed on harming others, other things being equal, is pretty uncontroversial, but the issue of causing offence is much more clouded. It can be argued, plausibly, that offence is a kind of harm, but because this is controversial and nothing hinges on it, we will assume that it is not. Nothing hinges on it because if offence is considered a kind of harm, then the issue is whether or not *that* sort of harm is something about which we ought to worry.

Assuming that offence is not harm, should activities that cause offence but not harm be restricted? This question is particularly important to discussions of freedom on the Internet, because giving offence by words or pictures is a common way of doing things that others might not like. One is tempted to say that if something merely gives offence there ought to be no restrictions placed on it. Too much would be ruled out if we were not allowed to offend people. People can be offended by almost anything, and frequently there is no way to tell in advance if something will be offensive. Prohibiting the giving of offence per se would almost certainly rule out the freedom to express opinions, particularly on matters that people see as personally important, like sex, politics, and religion, and that are likely to offend at least one person who may be overly sensitive, insecure, and so on. Because of its importance for the discussion of censorship of the Internet we will examine this notion in the following section.

GIVING OFFENCE

It was suggested in the previous paragraph that one is tempted to say that giving offence should not be reason in itself to curtail freedom of speech. But perhaps this is a bit swift. First, what is offence? Offence is a kind of unhappiness, mental distress, or some other sort of suffering. If I am offended my feelings are hurt in some way. If we want to live harmoniously with others, we ought to avoid causing any kind of suffering, other things being equal. Giving offence, however, is not quite the same as causing physical harm. I can harm someone by offending that person only if he or she *takes* offence. Perhaps people only take offence if they are overly sensitive or if they hold certain beliefs quite dearly. Therefore, in a sense, if they are hurt by something said, it is their own fault. But this is still too swift.

Two questions emerge: (1) What, if anything, is wrong with giving offence, and (2) Why do people take offence? In answer to (1), one may be inclined to say that there is nothing really wrong with giving offence. After all, if people are so silly or sensitive that they become hurt at something said, so much the worse for them. We cannot spend all of our lives worrying about who might not like what we say. While this line of thought contains an element of truth, it is a bit hard. It is probably true that any offence taken at the mocking of a football team is not normally taken too seriously, but the mocking of a physical disability or a tragedy, for example, might not only be in bad taste, but also extremely hurtful even for those not overly sensitive. We are, after all, human. And even if no offence is taken in the sense of feelings or pride being hurt, it might be that painful memories are awakened. However, not all offence is of this type. People are offended by blasphemy, language to do with sexual activity, ridicule of race, class, occupation, political belief, and a host of other things. And while some of these seem not too worrisome, others do.

Before proceeding with an answer to (1), we will look at (2)—why people take offence. Obviously, offence is taken for different reasons by different people and over a wide range of areas. Here we will look at four areas, the first of which concerns things that are not necessarily directed at any person or group, such as sexually explicit language and nudity (and not necessarily pornography). Some people are offended by certain language and pictures. Part of the explanation for the offence taken clearly has to do with upbringing and socialisation. But this is not a complete explanation. Why offence rather than anger? There might be anger when something is not liked because it is thought that it will have harmful consequences, for example, that it will contribute to the corruption of youth or the general lowering of community standards. Offence seems to involve something more than this. If I find something offensive I take it personally in some way. I am *hurt*, not just angered. A reasonable explanation of why I am hurt is that I identify closely with the belief that this sort of behaviour is wrong, and in a way, I feel violated. If you expose me to these things that you know I do not like, then you are not showing me the respect that I deserve as a person. Even if it was not directed at me in particular, I may feel that people like me are not respected enough. In both cases we may feel devalued as persons.

The second area is the ridicule or even just criticism of beliefs and commitments, particularly perhaps religious and political. A reason that offence is taken here is that we tend to identify with a set of beliefs or with a group in a way that makes those beliefs or that group part of our self-image. So when ridicule is directed at those beliefs or that group, we feel that we are being ridiculed, and again can feel that we are not being respected as persons. The third area is the offence taken at language that is racist or sexist or makes fun of or otherwise denigrates those with mental or physical disabilities or the victims of accidents or crimes. What these examples all share is the fact that there is no choice involved in being a member of any of these groups. There is a real sense here in which our identity and self-image is inextricably bound up with the group of which we find ourselves members. Offence will almost always be bound up with self-respect. The fourth and final area has to do with integrity. It is easy to take offence if our integrity is questioned. In a recent case in Australia, the honesty of an international aid agency was questioned. In a letter to past contributors it was stated that "our dedicated staff have been deeply offended by the allegations made." The questioning of someone's integrity is the questioning of what people see themselves as being.

In all of these cases we find that there is a close connection between the taking of offence and self-respect or esteem. When someone makes a remark that we find offensive, we feel that we are not being respected as humans. Our self-respect may be lessened to some extent. Too many of these comments can cause us to see ourselves as people of little worth. If something that is an integral part of me is ridiculed, such as my height, race, or intelligence, this is evidence that others do not value me as a person. They are not showing me the respect that I deserve as a person. If I identify very closely with a football team or with a religion and if that team or religion is ridiculed, I may feel the same way. So perhaps we can say that what is wrong with giving offence in general is the lack of respect it shows for others, possibly causing them to lose some of their self-respect.

Lack of respect may be objectionable for reasons other than its possible effect on self-respect, but this possible effect should be taken seriously. It is important to note that the respect under consideration is respect for *persons*, as distinct from respect for a *role* occupied by a person. I might show little respect for someone as a professor for example, but still respect him or her as a person. This is not a sharp distinction, particularly in societies in which people are to a large extent identified with their occupations, but can be a viable one. If someone shows me lack of respect as a person, and if I recognise this, it is difficult for my self-respect not to be dented. However, if I am not respected as a professor by someone who believes that universities ought to be places for the totally free exchange of ideas with no academic hierarchy, there is nothing to take as a personal slight.

This account fits in with commonly held beliefs in two respects. First, it explains why offence connected with race and physical disability, for example, seems to be much more serious than offence related to football allegiances or sexually explicit language. If we choose to make a commitment to something, we should be prepared, to some extent anyway, to accept the consequences of making that commitment. At any rate, there is an important difference between areas in which we have some choice, like football team allegiance, and those in which we do not, such as race.

Not all cases are clear-cut, of course. Religious belief is a good example. That there is some choice possible in religious commitment is obvious. People do choose to join or leave particular religious groups. But religious beliefs are also closely connected with culture, and we do not have much choice as to the culture in which we find ourselves. This perhaps partly explains why offence at criticism or ridicule of religious beliefs is often so deep. Our culture helps make us what we are, and so do our religious beliefs. Mature, thinking adults, however, cannot plausibly maintain that they have no choice in their religious beliefs. They may have had no choice in the faith in which they grew up, but once mature and aware of other faiths, the choice is there to abandon their original beliefs. So criticism of the religious beliefs of a university-educated person is not necessarily showing any lack of respect, while doing the same to an uneducated peasant who has had no real opportunity to choose, may be. In the former case it may even be showing respect, in that we consider the person to be mature and intelligent enough to be able to cope with criticism.

The second way in which this account of offence fits in with common beliefs is that it also helps to explain why it seems more objectionable to mock or ridicule the disadvantaged than the advantaged. If someone takes offence at some mockery of an advantaged group, that person must first identify himself or herself with that group, that is, they must see themselves as privileged in some way. If they can only take offence to the extent that they identify with some favoured section of society, they are unlikely to have their self-respect dented. And if it is, does it matter?

CENSORSHIP OF THE INTERNET

We will now apply the previous discussion to censorship problems as they arise on the Internet. Concerns about material on the Internet can roughly be grouped into four areas: pornography, hate language, information to aid harmful activities, and "virtual harm."

Questions of free speech and censorship probably arise most frequently in connection with pornography. While anything available on the Internet would also be available elsewhere, or at least material of the same type would be, the situation is slightly different simply because it is so much more difficult to control the material put on the Internet and its distribution. Anybody can put anything on, and with varying degrees of difficulty, almost anybody can have access to it. In addition, gaining access to pornography on the Internet may be a very private affair. Locked in one's room, one can browse and search to one's heart's content. There is no need to face the possible embarrassment of detection in buying or hiring material from a newsagent or video shop, or the interception of mail. As a consequence, it is much more difficult to restrict Internet use to adults. And the most popular kind of pornography seems not to be of the "nicest" kind: "The biggest demand is not for hard-core sex pictures but for deviant material including paedophilia, bondage, sadomasochism and sex acts with various animals" (Elmer-Dewitt 1995: 50).

The second main area of concern is hate language, usually racist language. Particular groups, especially white supremacy groups, spread their messages of hate, free from any control, in a way not normally possible using other media. The third area is the imparting of information designed to cause harm to other people. A common example mentioned is information on how to construct bombs. Another is advice on how to abduct children for the purpose of molestation. It might be argued that this is nothing new, that this information is available anyway, possibly in the local public or university library. This may be so, but again it is much easier to get it in the privacy of one's room than in a public place.

Finally, there is the question of "virtual harm." By virtual harm we do not mean something fake or something that does not cause real suffering. This harm is real, but in a virtual world. The best known example of this is the "rape" of a woman in a virtual world. The rape is not real in the sense of being physical, bodily harm, but given the sort of communication and contact that occurs in a virtual world, in this case a MOO, the harm and suffering is real. (A MOO, for our purposes, is a "place" on the Internet where people can interact with each other in real time.) Rape in the real world has nothing to do with censorship, so why should virtual rape? Simply because virtual rape is language based. The "rapist" uses language to inflict the suffering, so banning this sort of behaviour would amount to banning a certain kind of language, and hence censorship.

What then is different about censorship of the Internet? In a sense nothing is new. The same issues about freedom of speech and individual rights are present as in any discussion of the topic. But there are a few differences, some already alluded to. One is the ease of both spreading and receiving material. Another is the privacy possible in doing so. Yet another is the fact that the Internet is global in a sense in which other media are not. National and cultural borders are irrelevant. So if there is to be some control, from where will it emanate? Just how this can raise interesting problems even within one country is shown in the following quotation:

> [A California couple] were indicted for transmitting porno-graphic material to a government agent in Tennessee. A jury in Memphis wasted little time ruling that the images—which in-cluded pictures of women having sex with animals—were ob-scene. But [this] case raised the tricky constitutional question of which locale's community standards should have been used to make the judgment: Tennessee's Bible Belt, California's Bay Area or the virtual community of cyberspace? (Cole 1995: 53)

Should censorship be applied to the Internet? More specifically, should it be applied in any of the four areas mentioned previously? Opponents of censorship usually base their objections on arguments for freedom of ex-pression. But freedom of expression can mean different things, as we saw earlier. It might be the freedom to express opinions, the freedom to say anything at all, or most broadly, the freedom to express oneself in any way at all. How does this distinction affect the four areas of Internet concern? First, pornography has little to do with the freedom to express opinions, though probably a lot to do with freedom of expression in the wider senses. Second, hate language could fit into all three categories. It might be the expression of an opinion about some race or group, or it might merely be abuse. The imparting of information might be an expression of something, but hardly of an opinion. Virtual harm could certainly be the expression of something, but also not so plausibly of an opinion. In the Internet context it is related to the freedom to say anything.

Perhaps pornography should only be censored if it causes harm and not merely because it may offend, but we will say more about the question of censorship and offence shortly. Whether or not it does cause harm to adults is hotly debated. It is often claimed that pornography exploits those involved in its production, but of course much pornography is in written form, so that no actual person is involved, and with current tech-nology even photographs may be digitally manipulated in such a way that the original subject is unrecognisable, if there even was an original subject. Therefore, any idea that exploitation is necessarily involved in the production is unfounded. (See our discussions of manipulating images in chapter 3 and virtual sex in chapter 10.) The issue then is whether or not pornography has harmful effects on its consumers.

While it may be agreed that adults' access to pornography should not be prohibited, the case might be different with children. We do protect our children from all sorts of things, from not only actual harm, but also pos-sible harm. One way to protect children from pornography is to ban it altogether from the Internet. Even if this were possible, which it probably is not, it would be a bit drastic. A better approach would be to make it difficult for children to get access to it, a solution possible in various ways. Now of course another problem arises. Why should children be subject to censorship? Luckily this issue can be avoided here. Software is readily available that can filter out material parents, teachers, or other guardians of children may not want their charges to see or read. So the issue of children's censorship on the Internet raises no questions that do not arise in censoring children's reading in any other medium.

How does freedom of expression affect hate language? If it occurs in the expression of an opinion it may be tolerable on Millian grounds, but much of it is just abuse, insult, or worse. This is more difficult to defend than pornography. While the freedom to express opinions, even if those opinions might cause suffering, can promote other goods, it is unclear that the freedom to abuse and so on does any good at all. It is difficult to see how it could help to promote truth or a better way of life. It is certainly offensive, but that in itself is not enough to justify censoring it. More extreme uses of racist language, for example, can probably cause harm to those at whom it is directed, particularly if it occurs over an extended period of time. The harm is likely to be the lowering or loss of self-respect. If this is so, a strong case could be made for placing restrictions on this sort of language.

The placing of dangerous information on the Internet, for example, instructions for bomb making or tactics for terrorism, can clearly not be defended on the grounds of freedom of expression. Such information may well cause harm, whether intended or not. As has already been seen, while freedom of expression is good and useful, limits must be placed on it. We cannot be free to express ourselves in ways that harm others. The case of virtual harm might seem obvious, depending on how this harm is viewed. If it is real, then freedom of expression cannot be used to defend actions that cause it. On the other hand, if it is not real, then it is not a problem. It is necessary then to look a bit more carefully at what this virtual harm is. The best-known example is the publicised rape in LambdaMOO (Dibbell 1994). It was not a real rape because nothing physical happened—it all occurred through language. However, because of the context, real suffering was caused, real, that is, in the sense of affecting people in the real world and not just in the virtual world. So, it might be argued, just as in the real world rape is not allowed as a form of expression, so virtual rape should not be allowed on the Internet either. But the notion of rape or any other physical harm does not make much sense on the Internet as a whole. It makes more sense, though, in the restricted context of LambdaMOO or some other MOO. LambdaMOO is essentially the context for a game in which players take on personalities and interact is various ways with one another. In this context, rape and other crimes make sense, as does suffering, although the suffering appears to extend beyond the confines of the game. A strong case could be made for prohibiting such verbal behaviour from a MOO, but that is different from prohibiting it from the whole Internet. Language that might be interpreted as rape in the context of a game is not rape in any sense outside the game, even if it is offensive. But offence per se is not enough to justify censorship.

Mill, as we saw, defends freedom of expression. This freedom helps people choose the lifestyle that best suits them and helps overcome the "tyranny of custom." To what extent do his arguments support freedom on the Internet? Pornography, hate language, and virtual harm can all be expressions of lifestyle. However, the latter two at least also cause harm to others and so violate his "harm to others" principle. The spreading of dangerous information gains little support because it has little to do with expression in the required sense.

Finally, what can be said about offence and censorship on the Internet? The account presented earlier of what is wrong with giving offence allows us to draw some lines in the clash between freedom of speech and restrictions on giving offence. It is of course not only impractical to place a ban on the giving of offence, it is also blatantly silly. Very little at all could be said, given the possibility of the potential audience containing someone with acute sensibilities. But a concentration on respect for persons rather than on offence itself is more helpful. Mill argues, as already seen, that one of the strengths of freedom of speech is that it forces people to continually reexamine their beliefs, and that as a result, those beliefs, or the ones that survive, will be stronger and more lively. Beliefs unexamined wither and die. On these grounds, freedom of speech overrides worries about giving offence in the case of ridiculing or criticising beliefs and commitments. The same argument can apply to the case in which certain language or pictures are taken as offensive in themselves. To the extent that such language or pictures might be seen as offensive because of beliefs, these beliefs should be open to challenge. To the extent that the offence is not based on beliefs but purely on something like taste, it seems unimportant. This suggests that offence is no reason for censoring pornography.

Mill's dictum does not apply when the offence concerns race, appearance, or other factors over which we have no control. No amount of freedom of speech is going to change my race or appearance, even if I want it to. A plausible argument can be made that freedom of speech ought to be restricted when it harms or is likely to harm someone's self-respect by showing a lack of respect to a person or group. Offensive hate language would be a case in point. Whether an attack on a person's integrity is wrong really depends on the justification for the attack. While accusations of dishonesty, for example, can be associated with a lack of respect for a person, if the evidence is strong, this lack of respect may be justified. In the interests of justice, freedom of speech cannot be curtailed.

Offence, in summary, is a relevant consideration in censorship, but only in those areas in which self-respect is at stake. Pornography should not normally be restricted on the grounds of offence, nor should dangerous information or language causing virtual harm. Any of these of course may fall foul of other principles.

It is sometimes thought that if something offends almost everyone, then offence is a good reason for censorship. But it is unclear why this should be so. Why should it be relevant that a large number of people rather than a small number are offended by something? And again, it may be that there is value in offending the vast majority. Questioning a deeply held belief in a society might offend almost everyone, but it may also force them to think more carefully about that belief and to reject it, modify it, or hold it in a more active fashion.

There are a couple of other issues of relevance when we talk of censorship on the Internet. We will assume that censorship in various instances is justified, for example, the censorship of racial hate language. However, it still might *not* be justified to censor it on the Internet, as distasteful as it is. Censoring such language in newspapers is one thing; it is quite another to censor it in private communication. Much Internet communication is private, frequently on a one-to-one basis. Such communication normally ought to remain private and it is an invasion of privacy to monitor such communication. (There may be some exceptions, for example in national security and criminal investigation matters.) General discussions of censorship usually do not concern censorship of private mail or private conversation, and this ought to apply to the Internet as well. This is the first issue. The second concerns practicability. Effectively censoring activity on the Internet will not be easy to do without limiting its usefulness. While it may not be good that certain sorts of things are communicated, such as things that may harm some people, it may well be worse overall if this form of communication is restricted in ways that would limit the effectiveness of the Internet. It is difficult to see how it would be possible, given current technology, not to throw out too many babies with the bath water.

SUMMARY

In this chapter we have tried to sort out some of the important theoretical issues having to do with censorship on the Internet. First, "freedom of speech" is ambiguous. It can refer to the freedom to express opinions, or to expression in a wider sense. This distinction is important in discussions of censorship, because it is often attacked on the grounds that freedom of opinion is a good thing. However, much material that is the subject of debate with respect to censorship has nothing to do with the expression of opinion. It has to do with expression, but not necessarily of an opinion. Second, the arguments for both freedom of opinion and freedom of expression of other sorts were considered, and these were applied to each of four areas that have become the subject of discussions of censorship of the Internet: pornography, hate language, harmful information, and virtual harm. The conclusion was that tolerating some forms of hate language could be justified on the grounds of freedom of opinion, but that such grounds do not extend to the other three areas. Finally, it was argued that while offence is important in discussions of censorship, it should only be used as a reason for censorship when it may cause a loss of self-respect. The freedom of expression can only be overridden if harm is caused to others. Censorship of Internet pornography is not justified, except perhaps in the case of children. Censorship of certain kinds of hate language and of harmful instructions could be justified. Language that causes virtual harm could be censored in individual contexts, but not on the Internet as a whole. Finally, we looked at the bigger picture and suggested that given current technology, more might be lost than gained by restricting freedom of speech on the Internet.

REFERENCES

ALA Code of Ethics. 1995. [On-line]. Available gopher://gopher.ala.org:70/00/alagophii/ethics.txt

Cole, Wendy. 1995. The Marquis de Cyberspace. *Time* 27 [Australia] (July 10): 53.

Dibbell, Julian. 1994. Data rape: A tale of torture and terrorism on-line. *Good Weekend: The Age Magazine* [Melbourne, Australia] (19 February): 26–32.

Elmer-Dewitt, Philip. 1995. On a screen near you: Cyberporn. *Time* 27 [Australia] (July 10): 48–55.

Giles, Richard. 1990. Are there times when censorship is justified? In *For and against: Public Issues in Australia*, ed. Richard Giles. Milton, Qld: Brooks Waterloo, p. 61.

Hauptman, Robert. 1988. *Ethical Challenges in Librarianship*. Phoenix, AZ: Oryx Press.

Mill, John Stuart. 1859. *On Liberty*; page citations to edition of David Spitz, 1975.

"The Universal Declaration of Human Rights." *Human Rights Manual*. 1993. Canberra: Australian Government Publishing Service, pp. 137–42.

FURTHER READING

Feinberg, Joel. 1983. *The Moral Limits of the Criminal Law*. 4 vols. New York: Oxford University Press.

Long, Robert Emmet, ed. 1990. *Censorship*. The Reference Shelf, vol. 62, no. 3. New York: H. W. Wilson.

Orr, Lisa, ed. 1990. *Censorship: Opposing Viewpoints*. San Diego, CA: Greenhaven Press.

5

Intellectual Property

Why bother to create something if it is to be stolen? . . . Why bother if I can't own my own words and have that recognised throughout the world as my original creation? . . . There is a quantum difference between printed and electronic publishing. Electronic texts can be used in secret by people thousands of kilometres away from their source. Even worse, they can be entered and altered, sabotaged and filched, so that no one may ever know it happened and how. The Internet has no quality control and its vast scale makes it impossible to police by peer review. . . . Copyright for academics goes to the heart of our scholarly and scientific enterprise. It is the cornerstone of all learning. And if the universities do not recognise and defend the concept and practice of copyright they could self-destruct. (McCalman 1995: 9, 11)

As we work today to rethink about how to encourage learned men (and women) to compose and write useful books, it may be helpful to realize that copyright is a social construct that has been and should be tailored to achieve the purposes we have for it. It is not some predestined, static law of humankind. (Samuelson 1995: 17)

The idea of property comes up in a number of areas in computer and information ethics. If there is a worry about software piracy, it is because there is a belief that someone legitimately owns the software, and illegal copying amounts to theft of property. Documents, images, and data are also considered to be owned in many cases, that is, they are the property of someone. Most people, at least those in the Western world, think that they have a right to own things. The main interest here is in intellectual property, that is, in the ownership of ideas (actually it is something like the *expression* of ideas, but for our purposes this does not matter), but it will be useful first to consider property in general.

PROPERTY IN GENERAL

Why do we think that private property is justified and is a good thing? This might sound like an odd question now, but not so long ago it was frequently raised, and in fact the justification of intellectual property is still quite hotly debated. In the last century Karl Marx wrote:

> *Communism* is the *positive* abolition of *private property*, of *human self-alienation*, and thus the real *appropriation* of *human* nature through and for man. It is, therefore, the return of man to himself as a *social*, i.e. really human, being, a complete and conscious return which assimilates all the wealth of previous development. (1844: 136)

Probably the most famous justification of property in general comes from John Locke. He argued that if one "mixed one's labour" with something then one had a legitimate claim to it:

> Though the Earth, and all inferior Creatures be common to all Men, yet every Man has a *Property* in his own *Person*. . . . The *Labour* of his Body, and the *Work* of his Hands, we may say, are properly his. Whatsoever then he removes out of the State that Nature hath provided . . . he hath mixed his *Labour* with, and joyned to it something that is his own, and thereby makes it his *Property*. . . . For this *Labour* being the unquestionable Property of the Labourer, no Man but he can have a right to what that is once joyned to, at least where there is enough, and as good left in common for others (1689: 328–29, section 27)

It must be noted that Locke placed some restrictions on the right to appropriate goods. There had to be, for example, enough left for others. But the basic thrust of this justification of property is that if I build a house, it is mine because my labour is mixed with it. Something of me is in the house. The main weakness in Locke's argument, as Robert Nozick (1980: 175) points out, is that it is not obvious why we should gain what we mix our labour with, rather than simply losing our labour. If I poured a can of tomato juice, which I owned, into the sea, would I own the sea or just lose my juice? The answer is obvious.

Another argument frequently used today is the utilitarian one that private ownership is necessary as an incentive to work. This dates back to

David Hume, who argued that a person's creations should be owned by him or her to encourage "useful habits and accomplishments." This is the argument most often appealed to in support of intellectual property. The comment of Marx and Engels on this justification is worth noting:

> It has been objected that upon the abolition of private property all work will cease, and universal laziness will overtake us. . . . According to this, bourgeois society ought long ago to have gone to the dogs through sheer idleness; for those of its members who work, acquire nothing, and those who acquire anything, do not work. (1848: 48)

Their argument is that the working class who do all of the work do not get property, while the capitalists who acquire all the property do not work.

Another justification is based on desert. A producer or creator deserves reward for his or her production or creation. If I create something I deserve something in return for my effort. Nothing follows necessarily of course about ownership, but ownership is often thought to be a just reward. It might in some cases be a just reward, but it is not the only one and perhaps not the best one or the one that the creator wants. The creator may prefer gratitude or recognition to ownership (see Hettinger 1989: 40–43)

INTELLECTUAL PROPERTY

The Universal Declaration of Human Rights says in Article 27 (2), "Everyone has the right to the protection of the moral and material interests resulting from any scientific literary or artistic production of which he is the author" (1993: 141).

Both the ACM and the ALA in their respective codes of ethics also endorse the right to intellectual property. The ACM code states that a member will "Honour property rights including copyrights and patents" (1.5), while the ALA code says "We recognize and respect intellectual property rights" (iv). No justification is given of intellectual property rights. Perhaps it is just obvious. We just do have a right to what we create. But this is not satisfying—we want to know why.

Intellectual property is interestingly different from other property. Owning an idea, or something abstract, is not simply like owning a physical object. Ownership of a physical object comes about, in our culture, through either making it, being given or sold it by the previous owner, or, within certain restrictions, finding it. And ownership involves the right to continued use and enjoyment of it; if it is a painting, for instance, and I take it from your house without your authority, my theft of it consists in my violation of that right because you are no longer able to have that use and enjoyment.

There is another interesting aspect to intellectual property that distinguishes it from other property. In what sense or to what extent is an idea mine? If I build or buy a house, I know what is mine. If I either provide all of the labour and materials, or pay for everything myself, it is my house, other things being equal. But an idea is not like this, even if the article, painting, or software that is its manifestation was written or painted by me. Ideas may come from anywhere, and probably any idea that we have is not ours alone. Most of my ideas come from someone else. At best, when I am "original," I express an idea in a new way, I see associations between ideas not noticed before, I see the relevance of an idea in some situation, or I combine ideas in a new way. While these factors can all be significant, in all of them anything creative that I achieve is the adding of something to preexisting ideas that I have obtained from others. So to what extent is the new idea really mine? Given that I contributed only a little, why should I claim ownership? If I contribute a little to your house, perhaps I can claim that I own a little, morally anyway, but certainly not that I own the whole house. Similarly, if I write a book, most of the ideas will have come from elsewhere (most of the ideas in *this* book came from elsewhere), so why should I be able to claim ownership?

What does the ownership of intellectual property amount to? In our terms, what is involved in the ownership of a digital image, a piece of writing, or computer software? If you create a digitally stored image, text, or software and I steal it by copying it onto my disk or into my area of the computer, you still have that image, in contrast to the case of the stolen painting. What I now have is a copy of what you have. This is an important difference between intellectual property and other property. Intellectual property is not exclusive. My use of it does not exclude your use. Intellectual property rights do not grant exclusive use and enjoyment of that owned. They are concerned more with financial gain, which is restricted primarily to the owner. So the main issue is not taking something from the owner or creator and thereby depriving her of access to it, but rather it is the copying of the work or software.

First, what is wrong with the unauthorised copying of the work of another? One answer is simply that it is an infringement of ownership rights. While this violation of rights might be spelt out in terms having nothing to do with consequences, perhaps in a Lockean manner (and we will return to this later), more typically it would be cashed in terms of harm or potential harm to the owner. The owner loses in some way as a result of the copying, just as owners lose in theft. Copying is seen as a kind of theft; the theft of an idea. We will first consider grounds for intellectual property that are based on harm (or the associated notion of incentive), and then other grounds.

An owner of intellectual property is deemed to lose if the property is copied, in terms of the ability to sell the idea or perhaps in terms of prestige or promotion. If I have a good idea, paint a good picture, take an interesting photograph, or develop good and novel software, I want people to know that it is mine, and so, perhaps, gain in one or more of the ways just mentioned. If copying were freely allowed, there would be no money to be made, and profits must be available or nobody will make the effort to develop their ideas. Or at least that is the claim. So the issue is essentially one of harm, both to the individual owner and to society in general.

Before commenting further on this, we will consider the question in another way: When is it legitimate to copy the work of another? At one end of the spectrum lies the case in which a work is copied and passed off as the work of another for commercial gain. At the other end might be the scanning of an image from a magazine solely for the purpose of experimenting with morphing. Or it might be using clip art to create a new image or copying software purely to see how it works, without any intention of using it without buying it. What are the main differences between the two ends of the spectrum? In the first, the copier gains financially at the expense of the owner and there is deceit involved. In the second case, no financial gain is made from the copying, or at least, none that affects the owner of the work. And no deceit is involved. The copier can quite happily acknowledge the source of the work or software if the need arises. Harm, particularly financial, is again an issue, and so is deceit. Harm will be examined now and deceit later.

Financial harm caused to the owner is a reason then why copying is wrong. But it is not so simple. Harming anyone unnecessarily and intentionally, either physically or emotionally, is generally accepted as unethical. But harming someone financially is not so obviously wrong, even though theft and robbery are not usually considered to be desirable activities. The possibility of financial harm, in fact, is built into the free market system. It is argued that having a free market is better overall than not having one, even though some people will suffer. So harming someone financially is not generally considered unethical in itself. But financial harm does play a part in the argument, which goes roughly like this: The generation of new ideas is necessary for a society to prosper. It can be time consuming and costly to generate and develop ideas, so there must be reward for those who do. If there is not, nobody will bother to create. And the most important reward is financial. Without financial reward, society's supply of new ideas will dry up. Therefore, there must be some system of copyright and patent regulations to protect intellectual property. So one argument against copying then, from the perspective of harm, is the harm caused to society at large if there were no restrictions on the practice.

Whether it is in fact true that without financial reward there would be no incentive to create, is another matter. In medieval times all literature was in the public domain, with no ownership rights. "Story material . . . was looked upon as common property and the notion that one could claim property rights in ideas is seldom encountered" (Malone and Baugh 1967: 114). It could be thought of course that the medievals were not very original, but it would still need to be shown that even if this was so, it was a result of the lack of the concept of intellectual ownership.

It could be argued, on the other side of the ledger, that if ideas were all in the public domain, and if anyone could work on and develop anything regardless of where the idea originated, we would all be better off because more would be developed. That the source of new and innovative ideas would dry up without copyright and patent laws to facilitate financial reward is little more than an article of faith. Artists, academics, and scientists frequently create without such reward. Perhaps acknowledgement is enough. Or perhaps creation is its own reward.

The most that this discussion questions of course, is whether society in general suffers from copying others' work, not whether individuals will be harmed by having their work copied. This can certainly happen in our present social structure. Individual harm must be taken into account even if society as a whole would be better off with no restrictions on copying. But it is not an overriding consideration. As we have already noted, some individuals suffer in a free market economy, but it is the current wisdom that such an economy is still better than the alternatives.

Is there anything wrong with copying when no harm is involved, for example the copying of material that one would never buy? Here the owner is not harmed. There is no financial loss because there was no question of the work being purchased. The owner may in fact benefit, given that he or she gets more exposure. But we are still reluctant to say that this copying is moral. Why? A Lockean justification would go like this: If I create something, it is mine simply because it is a product of my intellectual labour. If my labour is mixed with an image, a text, or with software, that is, if I painted or drew it or took the photograph, wrote the text or the program, then it is my property. I have rights over it because something of me, namely my labour, is in it. So if anyone copies or alters my work without my permission, they are violating my rights. Whether these actions are moral or not has nothing to do with their consequences. The actions are immoral even if the consequences for others are good.

While this type of justification is not universally accepted and does have problems, as we noted earlier, it is *prima facie* a reasonable account of why we have intellectual property rights. It does of course still have the problem mentioned in the general discussion of property, that is, why do we gain that with which we mix our labour? An alternative justification is that the creator just *deserves* some reward for having an idea and developing it. This has some intuitive appeal, but it does not justify ownership.

There are many ways in which one could be rewarded for creating or producing something without being given ownership over it. One could be paid in money or given a long holiday!

APPLICATIONS OF INTELLECTUAL PROPERTY

So far we have considered how property rights, in particular intellectual property rights, can be justified. Attention will now turn to three areas in which the property issue rears its head. The first has to do with digital images, the second with online searching, and the third with computer software piracy. These areas all raise questions of intellectual property and of copyright, and all deserve discussion, but only the last one has received much attention in the press.

DIGITAL IMAGES REVISITED

In a previous chapter we considered questions of freedom connected with the manipulation of images. The potential moral problems of interest now are questions of ownership.

Manipulation and the Ownership of Images

Ownership is a relevant issue in manipulation in two ways. The first has to do with the right to manipulate. Does ownership entail the right to manipulate? While the answer to this might seem obvious—of course that right is entailed—the issue is muddied by the fact that the notion of image ownership is not straightforward, both because intellectual property is significantly different from material property and because of problems with the idea of a copy and of copying. The second issue concerns the ownership of manipulated images. If I change an image that was digitised from a photograph or a picture drawn by someone else, whose property is the new image?

Ownership of Copies

If I own a copy of an image, what do I own? If I own a copy of the book *Oscar and Lucinda,* what I own is quite different from what the author, Peter Carey, owns. He owns some intellectual "thing," whereas I own an object made of paper containing words. I have no say in who can legitimately copy my copy, while he has. (Publisher's and author's rights will be combined here.) While I might legitimately own a copy of *Oscar and Lucinda,* I in no sense own the intellectual content. The same is true with an electronic image. I can own the image in the sense that I can use it for my own personal enjoyment, but I do not own the idea that is the image. That, in some important sense, remains the property of the creator.

Ownership and the Right to Manipulate

We now turn to the question of whether there are instances in which copying is legitimate but manipulation of the copied image is not. In other words, is licence to copy licence to manipulate? There are three cases to consider. The first is the case in which the copier has the right to make a copy but not to grant that right to others. He can legitimately make a copy for his own private purposes, but the image is still owned by someone else. This is essentially the case with photocopying text. The second case is exemplified when someone copies an image that they unquestionably own because it was either bought or received as a gift. This is the case in which someone buys all rights to an old movie or inherits all rights to a novel, for example. The third case is that in which the owner has all rights by virtue of being the creator. These will now be discussed in turn.

Is licence to copy the work of another, licence to manipulate that work? What can I do with the copy? Pretty well anything I like, providing that it is for my own personal use. The problems arise if I want to make the image, or some variant of it, public. But perhaps the issues are not much different from those arising in the case of written material. Suppose I manipulate my copy of the image owned by X and make it public. The issues are: What sort of changes have been made? How substantial are the changes? Have I acknowledged the source of the image? Have I made it clear that it is a manipulated image? Is it being used for research or for personal gain? (This is not a clear-cut distinction, as any publication can be for both purposes.) It is generally accepted that there is nothing wrong with using the work of others in published work as long as what is used is not too substantial, recognition is given to the copied work, and so on. After all, all research is to a greater or lesser extent building on the work of others. So there seems to be no good reason why the same situation should not obtain in the case of images. If I legitimately copy an image that I see as the basis for some other creation, and create the new from the old, it is difficult to see what is wrong with this, providing that due recognition is given to the creator of the original image.

But, it might be objected, just because I have a right to copy someone's work, it does not follow that I have a right to change it. If I have a right to copy X's work, then the copy that I make is mine. But it is not mine in the same sense that X's house is mine if I acquire it legitimately. If I acquire his house I can do what I like with it, more or less, because it is mine. Being mine in this case means that I own it. But I do not own my copy of X's image in that way. All that I own is the paper on which it is printed. It is still

X's image. Intellectual property is different from other property. Ownership of ideas is not much like the ownership of objects. X can sell me an idea that is made manifest in an image created by him, but there is a very real sense in which it is still his image, his idea.

While it is true that my legitimate copy of X's image is still in a sense his image, the sense in which it is, is not one that prevents me from altering it. If a copy of an image is changed, nothing happens to the original, and, at least in the case of digitally stored images, the potential number of copies of this original is not diminished. The world does not lose anything by the alteration—in fact it gains. There are now two images where there was only one.

The second case to be considered is that in which someone has purchased or has been given all rights, including the right to say who can copy, to an image (or set of images as in a movie). In this case is manipulation justifiable? If, for example, rights to a black-and-white movie were purchased, would the new owner have the right to colourize it? It is not clear that he would. Ownership rights do not necessarily confer the right to alter. If I purchase a work of art can I alter it? Once something has certain aesthetic or historical significance, I do not have the moral right to alter it even if I did purchase all legal rights to it. Society's rights override those of the individual owner. However, the right to alter a digital image is not so easily overridden. Of course, a new owner of the Mona Lisa would not have the moral right to adorn the face with spectacles or give her grey hair. However, the right to alter a copy is different. As in the previous case, nothing is lost here, providing that the unaltered version remains intact. There is nothing reprehensible in tinting a black-and-white movie if an untinted version is still available. Providing that the owner does not destroy the original of a digital image, there is nothing wrong with manipulating copies.

The final case is that in which the original owner and creator of the image is the one who manipulates. Is this different? Perhaps. If Charles Rennie Macintosh altered one of his buildings in Glasgow, it would still be a Macintosh building. If a new owner alters it, it loses some of its significance. However, if the creation is significant enough, perhaps even the creator should not change it, if the change destroys the original. If the original is unchanged though, it is even more doubtful than in the two earlier cases that changing a copy is in any way wrong.

Ownership of Manipulated Images

A related question now is this: If I copy an image and manipulate it, is the resultant manipulated image mine, or does it still belong to the owner of the original? This problem is illustrated well in the recent lawsuit filed in New York City by the stockphoto agency FPG International against

New York Newsday. "Allegedly, someone at the newspaper scanned the work of two photographers . . . out of an FPG catalog and combined the images, plus some others, in the computer. Who got the credit for this new image? *New York Newsday*'s computer artist" (Russell 1994: 58).

Is ownership here a matter of having been authorised by the original owner to make the alterations? Does it make a difference if permission was granted for copying and manipulation? Perhaps it does. If I build a house completely out of stolen materials, the house is hardly mine, until at least I have adequately compensated the legitimate owners of the materials. It might be mine in the sense that I designed and created it, but no moral rights with respect to it would follow from this. The mere fact that I had put my labour into it would count for nought. However, if the materials were a gift, the house could be mine in all senses. Similarly perhaps, if manipulation was done with authority and with due reference, and if it was extensive enough to constitute a genuinely different picture, then I could legitimately claim it as mine. If that authority were lacking, I could not do so.

The cases are not parallel of course, and that makes a difference. The elements of an image used to create another image are not objects in the way that the constituents of a house are. In a sense they are intellectual objects, in another they are patches of colour, hence they can be used without depriving their owner of anything (providing that the original image is not destroyed). This is clearly not the case when house-building materials have been stolen. While creating a new image out of, and perhaps based on, the work of another may have "the benefit of theft over honest toil," it does not follow that this has any relevance for intellectual ownership. The foundations of this type of ownership might be built on sand, but insofar as good arguments could be given for the ownership rights of the original owner, they would also support the ownership of a manipulated image by the manipulator, regardless of whether permission had been granted.

ONLINE SEARCHING

The theft of information is an important issue, but much theft of information from computers raises no new moral questions. Taking information from an electronic database is not morally different from taking it from a card file or from anything else. But the case of online search results is more interesting, because there are several ethical issues related to this activity. The one of interest here is who owns or has rights over the information produced by the search. The accepted position is that the database vendor has rights that legitimately restrict what the customer can do with the data output.

> Under no circumstances may Customer, or any party acting
> by or through Customer, copy, transmit or retain data re-
> ceived from DIALOG Service in machine-readable form. . . .
> It is further agreed that data received from DIALOG Ser-
> vice, regardless of form, is not to be transferred, sold or in any
> manner commercially exploited, except as part of the ordi-
> nary attorney-client or library-patron relationship. (DIALOG
> 1990)

This statement by DIALOG makes it clear that I, as the customer, have
only very limited rights over the data output even if I conducted the
search myself. I cannot, for example, give that output to a colleague or a
student. Hauptman mentions this situation, but seems to imply that it is
merely onerous, and not morally unreasonable. "A strict interpretation of
copyright law mandates that it is illegal and unethical to download
searches that are requested frequently. Nor is it acceptable to retain duplicate hard copies to reuse them" (1988: 61). Why is it legitimate for vendors to make these claims? Hauptman provides an answer: "Unlike
publishers of manual indexes or general reference tools, database vendors earn their income through frequency of use. Each time a search is
performed, the vendor collects a fee, as well as royalties that revert to authors, database producers, or others" (1988: 61).

Hauptman's case study highlights a moral dilemma (1988: 61). An
online search coordinator completes an expensive search for a professor. Later, a student, in genuine financial hardship, requests the same
information. Should the coordinator (1) send the student to the professor, (2) give her a copy of the search, (3) charge her the normal price, or
(4) pay for the search himself? The important options here are (1) and
(2). The first concerns the issue of whether the professor could morally
pass on the information, while the second leaves the moral decision in
the hands of the coordinator. The fact that Hauptman raises this as a
moral dilemma suggests that he believes that in normal circumstances
search output should not be given to those who did not pay for the
search. We suggest that it is not obvious that vendors should be able to
place the restrictions that they do on the users of their databases. Search
outputs should have no more restrictions placed on them than do books
and other publications. To simplify matters, the assumption will be that
the user is the person who pays for and who conducts the search. That
this might not generally be the case does not affect any of the principles
discussed.

In a typical search situation the user will need to make a number of important decisions. She wants information on some topic, and typically she
wants all that is relevant, but not anything else. Getting all that is relevant

is not too difficult—just get everything. Getting only what is relevant is not so easy. The important point is that the user must have some knowledge both of searching strategies and of the field in which she wants the information. Suppose that her search is relatively successful. She gets more or less all and only what she wants. She can now use it for her own research or teaching, but she cannot give it to anyone else. Why is the situation different from that of a book? If she had bought a book containing the information, she would have been able to lend it to others or sell it as a used book. She cannot legally do either with the search output. Why is this so? One argument has to do with property rights. Vendors own the database because they have bought the information and put their labour into the construction of it. Therefore they have the right to say how it is used and how the output of it is used.

The problem with this ownership situation is that the user has also paid for the information. She paid the vendor for the privilege of doing the search. In addition, she contributed her labour to the search output by deciding what terms to use in the search. So she seems to have a legitimate claim to ownership of the output too. However, the vendor might say, the user only took from the database what was already there. She did not contribute to the content of the output. This is clearly not true. The content is a result of what was in the database and the user's choice and combination of search terms. The output that she achieved was not stored in the database in that form. But it might be objected that it was in the database implicitly, that all of the components were there. This is true, but suppose that the user reads a book, noticing various connections and relationships that the author does not. She writes them up and publishes her own book, giving due acknowledgment to the original book. The new book is hers, even if everything in it is implicitly in the old one. Her contribution is making explicit what was only implicit in the first work.

A utilitarian reason why the vendor might claim rights over the search output might also be given. Having databases is useful. They are expensive to build and maintain. Unless the vendors get a reasonable return for their efforts, there will be no databases. Given the structure of our society, they must make their profit from the users, so users must pay for the service. This might be true, but the argument is not that the users should not pay for the output. The argument is about what they are permitted to do with the output. It can then be claimed that the vendor is paid for each use, so the profit depends on the number of searches. If users are permitted to share or resell search output, vendors' profits will be cut, and eventually so will services. This, however, does not follow. Vendors may produce better services if they have to try harder to entice users to their services. And in any case, there will not normally be much demand for particular search results. People generally undertake online searching to find material on some particular interest of theirs. It is unlikely that many others will want just those specific results, so it is hard to see that profits would be much affected. Thus we have no good reasons for the restrictions that are in place on online search results.

SOFTWARE PIRACY

Software piracy is often thought of as simply the unauthorised copying of computer software. But copying software is not all of a kind. It can mean a number of different things, including the copying of actual code, the copying of the look and feel of some programs, and the copying of an algorithm. We will consider these in turn, in the light of our earlier discussion of property.

First, by the copying of actual code, we are referring to the making of electronic copies of commercial computer software. We are not interested in students copying someone's programming assignment. That is just cheating, and there is not much interesting to say about that. But even electronic copying of commercial software comes in a variety of forms, and not all of the moral issues are the same or necessarily have the same answers. The main differences concern the use to be made of the copy, which might sound odd. After all, surely theft is wrong, regardless of the use that is made of the stolen goods. But as we have already seen, stealing intellectual property is a little different from stealing other property. If I steal your software by copying it, I am not depriving you of its use. If I steal your car, I am.

Before considering the rightness or wrongness of unauthorised copying of software, we will look at some of the various uses made of the copies. First, there is copying in which the software is to be used for commercial gain, and, if it could not be copied, it would be purchased. In this case the owner is certainly harmed. A second case is that in which an individual copies a game, perhaps, that he would never bother buying, but thinks worth having if it's free. Here the owner is almost certainly not harmed. No sale has been lost. A third case concerns copying purely for testing, with the intention of buying if the product proves to be satisfactory.

There are obviously variations on these cases. For example, a group of students might share the cost of the software and then make copies, in a situation in which they cannot afford to buy individual copies. Or again, a university might copy some software that it requires for teaching because it cannot afford the payment that the owner wants for multiple copies. (No university in its right mind would do this, of course, even if only for legal reasons.) We will now look at the above three cases in more detail.

First, what about copying for commercial use? This does seem to be unjustifiable in general. It does deprive the owners of profit, and possibly harm them, although if they are very wealthy, the harm may be minimal. It is arguable of course that the real harm would be to society in general if this practice were too widespread, because less new software would be created if profits were low. And profits would be low if software were not bought. We have seen that the argument based on incentive is not always convincing, but it has some plausibility in this case. This is perhaps because in some ways software is more like a tool or a machine than like a novel, a work of art, or a research or scholarly article. In those cases the creative act in itself is some reward. Perhaps this is less so in the case of developing software. The creative act is in the design. The development, which includes testing, is much more tedious.

It is very dubious that the second example causes harm at all. If someone copies software that they would never have bought, even if it were inexpensive, the owner suffers no loss. And perhaps more importantly, the "but-what-if-everyone-did-this" objection carries no weight. If everyone who would never have bought the software copied it, the owner is still not harmed—still no sales are lost. So no case can be made here that the copying is wrong on the grounds that it causes harm. The situation is different if we mean "everyone" to include those who otherwise would have bought it. In this case the owner is harmed, so there is a reason for condemning that copying. But if the former kind of copying is wrong, that is, when the software would *not* have been bought, then it must be on the grounds of something such as the owner having the right to stop others from using his work, perhaps on the basis of desert. Pushing this line, however, makes the objection of the owner look a little petty. It amounts to saying that even though using my work without payment is not doing me any harm at all and is probably doing you some good, I do not want you to do so "because it is mine." We would probably want to scold a child for behaving like this!

The third case definitely seems not to be immoral, even if it is illegal. If I copy software purely for testing it, with the intention of buying if it satisfies my needs, I would be doing the owner a good turn. Buying without testing in most cases is just silly. Testing a copy is saving the owner the expense of providing me with a special copy for testing, a service practised by some. The owner has nothing to lose and something to gain by this activity of unauthorised copying for testing. There is perhaps a risk that I will keep the pirated copy rather than buying it, but if I do that then again I fall foul of the harm principle.

Copying the look and feel of a program is a little different from the previous cases. Here it is primarily the look of the user interface and perhaps the important functions of a program that are being copied. While the icons, the screen design, and so on may be identical or nearly so, the code may be quite different. This does seem to be much like copying someone else's idea, especially when the idea would normally be protected by a patent. Such theft does seem to be much like cheating, and as such perhaps ought to be condemned. The owner of the original product will quite likely be harmed if someone else develops similar software. There is no theft of code, but there is the taking of an idea. As well as harm to the owner, it could also be argued that without protection of the look and feel of a program, there will also be broader harm. Creators would be less willing to spend time, effort, and money on developing novel ideas if others could then develop similar products and so reduce the profits of the originators. The situation, though, is different from that in which the code is copied. There the copying is achieved with little more than the pressing of a few keys or a few clicks of a mouse button. In the look and feel case, the program must still be developed. It must be designed, programmed, and tested. So the copier must invest time, effort, and money into the project. Another relevant point is that it is beneficial to computer users if different software packages have similar user interfaces. These make programs "friendlier" and so easier to learn and use. Once one software package has been learnt, learning another is not too difficult. One has at least some idea of what to look for when learning something new. So it would seem that the disadvantages of copying the look and feel in disincentives to develop new products are more than outweighed by the advantages of having some standardisation and consistency among products. Again in this case, then, no very strong argument can be mounted for the immorality of copying on the grounds of harm and utility. Again if there is a strong case to be made, it must be based on rights or desert or the like.

Finally, is there anything wrong with copying a program algorithm? This issue is sometimes thought to revolve around the difference between discovery on the one hand and manufacture and creation on the other. The law reflects the view that we can, in some sense, own what we make or create, but not what we discover. As has been pointed out by Edwin Hettinger (1989), it seems more plausible to say "I own it because I made it" than to say "I own it because I discovered it." There are exceptions of course. Ownership of geographical territory has traditionally gone with discovery, when "discovery" is used in a very broad sense. But this is not generally applied. Discovering a law of nature does not give one ownership rights over it, and the same applies to mathematical formulae. Other cases are quite problematic. If I develop a recipe for a new drink, should I own that recipe? Did I create the new drink or did I discover it? In a sense I discovered it. All of the ingredients already existed. In another sense I created it by combining those ingredients in a way not done before. Suppose now that someone develops a cure for AIDS based on a new combination of ingredients. Here we seem more inclined to say that the cure was discovered than that it was created, but that might be simply because we have become accustomed to saying that penicillin and the like were discovered and extend that to all or most medical developments. But it does not seem to be the discovery aspect that makes private ownership objectionable here. It is rather that people's lives depend on these cures, and there is something obscene in anyone having the right to say who can have access to it simply on the grounds of discovery or even creation.

What has this to do with the right to own program algorithms? If algorithms are like laws of nature or like mathematical formulae, then they are discovered and so not able to be owned, or so the argument might go. But they are really more like recipes, in which the distinction between discovery and creation is much less clear. We certainly discover ways of doing things, and an algorithm is essentially a way of doing something, but there is also a sense in which we create or develop a way of doing things. What seems strange about claiming ownership for an algorithm is that it is saying that I should be the only person who is allowed to do something this way, or if anyone else does it this way, they ought to pay me simply because I thought of it first. Methods for doing something should not be owned. Perhaps a few people will spend less time and effort trying to find new ways of doing things, but surely this will be far outweighed by the fact that when new methods are found, everyone will be able to benefit by using them, and perhaps in some cases further develop them themselves.

SUMMARY

In this chapter we considered arguments for intellectual property and found that the justifications are not very strong; certainly not as strong as one would assume from popular discussions. It is not obvious that society is better off because of copyright and patent laws. The arguments based on harm and incentive contain a large portion of faith. The desert argument does not establish property rights, so we are left with a Lockean defence, which as we saw, is not problem-free either. Three computing and information topics in which some problems arise in connection with intellectual property were then examined. On the basis of the discussion at the beginning of the chapter, it was found that the questions of ownership of digital images, of the results of an online database search, and of computer software are problematic in many cases. It is much more difficult than is often admitted to make a strong case for intellectual ownership.

REFERENCES

DIALOG. 1990. *Terms and Conditions. DIALOG Classroom Instruction Program.*
Hauptman, Robert. 1988. *Ethical Challenges in Librarianship.* Phoenix, AZ: Oryx Press.

Hettinger, Edwin C. 1989. Justifying intellectual property. *Philosophy and Public Affairs* 18: 31–52.

Jordan, Z. A., ed. 1971. *Karl Marx: Economy, Class and Social Revolution*. London: Nelson.

Locke, John. 1689. *Second Treatise of Government*; page citations to the edition of Laslett, 1965.

Malone, K., and A. C. Baugh. 1967. *The Middle Ages*. London: Routledge & Kegan Paul.

Marx, Karl. 1844. *Economic and Philosophical Manuscripts*; page citations to edition of Jordan, 1971.

Marx, Karl, and Friedrich Engels. 1848. *Manifesto of the Communist Party*; page citations to 1971 edition, Moscow: Progress Publishers.

McCalman, Janet. 1995. Copyright and scholarship: Why it matters for academics. Unpublished paper, Melbourne.

Nozick, Robert. 1980. *Anarchy, State, and Utopia*. Oxford: Blackwell.

Russell, Anne M. 1994. Four Predictions: Who will win and who will lose, and will digital art ever get better? *American Photo* 5 (May/June): 58–59.

Samuelson, Pamela. 1995. Copyright and digital libraries. *Communications of the ACM* 38 (April): 15–21, 110.

The Universal Declaration of Human Rights. *Human Rights Manual. 1993*. Canberra: Australian Government Publishing Service, pp. 137–42.

FURTHER READING

Alexandra, Andrew. 1996. Computer networks and copyright. In *Issues in Computer Ethics*. Wagga Wagga, NSW: Keon Publications, pp. 1–11.

Forester, Tom. 1990. Software theft and the problem of intellectual property rights. *Computers and Society* 20 (March): 2–11.

Samuelson, Pamela. 1990. Should program algorithms be patented? *Communications of the ACM* 33 (August): 23–27.

Samuelson, Pamela. 1992. Copyright law and electronic compilations of data. *Communications of the ACM* 35 (February): 27–32.

Samuelson, Pamela. 1993b. Computer programs and copyright's fair use doctrine. *Communications of the ACM* 36 (September): 19–25.

Samuelson, Pamela. 1994. Copyright's fair use doctrine and digital data. *Communications of the ACM* 37 (January): 21–27.

Shaver, Donna B., Nancy S. Hewison, and Leslie W. Wykoff. 1985. Ethics for online intermediaries. *Special Libraries* 76 (Fall): 238–45.

Spinnello, Richard A. 1995. *Ethical Aspects of Information Technology*. Englewood Cliffs, NJ: Prentice Hall, chapter 6.

Steidlmeier, Paul. 1992. *People and Profits: The Ethics of Capitalism*. Englewood Cliffs, NJ: Prentice Hall.

Waldron, Jeremy. 1979. Enough and as good left for others. *Philosophical Quarterly* 29: 319–28.

Weil, Vivian, and John Snapper, eds. 1989. *Owning Scientific and Technical Information*. New Brunswick, NJ: Rutgers University Press.

6

Privacy

Confidential details about the private affairs of millions of ordinary people are routinely for sale on the black market, a *Sunday Times* investigation has revealed. . . . Within 48 hours, almost anything can be discovered about someone's life and social background: what car they drive, how much they spend, and where they eat, shop and go on holidays. (Hadfield and Skipworth 1993a)

[The] Midland Bank has approval to hold details about the sex lives of potential customers seeking insurance; BNFL is registered to store sexual and political information for "business and technical intelligence"; W. H. Smith, the high street retailer, has official sanction to hold sexual data for "personnel and employee administration" as well as for marketing purposes; Grand Metropolitan, the leisure company, is entitled to hold similar information for use by corporate lawyers; BT is licensed to hold information about political party membership "as a reference tool." (Hadfield and Skipworth 1993b)

Privacy is perhaps the most discussed ethical and social issue in computer and information technology. An article in *The Australian* newspaper of 14 March 1995, for example, had the headline "Privacy Issue to Dominate the '90s" (McIntosh 1995). The ACS (4.2), the ACM (1.7), and ALA (III) in their respective codes of ethics all talk of "respect" for the privacy of people. People are worried about the ease of the collection of personal data, its large-scale storage and easy retrieval, and about who can get access to it. They are also worried about the surveillance made easy by computer systems. Given its importance, why did we leave its discussion until halfway through the book? Because this is where it fits most logically. The discussion of privacy involves the notions of both freedom and property. Privacy is in part the freedom to do things away from the eyes and ears of others. It is also in part the ability to do what I like "in my own space," in my room, simply because it is mine.

Privacy is another of these things that we normally take for granted to be a good thing, but when we think about it a bit more carefully, it is not so clear just what it is and why it is so valuable. We will look first at the general questions and then turn to specific issues in the computer context. Of particular interest will be personal data and access to it, computer hacking as an invasion of privacy, and surveillance, especially in the workplace.

WHAT IS PRIVACY?

The word "privacy" is used in many different ways; it does not always mean the same thing. When we say that we want privacy we might mean any of the following, or something else:

I do not want other people in my room uninvited;

I do not want other people reading my mail, my diary, etc.;

I do not want others to know aspects of my past;

I do not want others to know some things that I do now;

I do not want others to see me in the bathroom;

I want to be able to be by myself.

What are normally considered to be private matters? First, our inner thoughts and feelings are our business only, and we are not obliged to talk of them to others. Commonly we resent it when others pry into these matters. Second, personal relationships are normally only private matters, at least in the sense that those involved want to be able to choose which third parties know details and which details they know. Third, other personal information, particularly about such aspects of our lives as our health and finances, are generally thought to be nobody else's business, except perhaps our doctors, accountants, and so on. We might not mind others knowing various things, but we want control over access to the knowledge. Fourth, we want our own space, to a greater or lesser degree. This space might be our own room, house, desk, or whatever (and not necessarily our "own" in the sense of private ownership). We like to be alone, which involves having control over who has access to us, at least sometimes. Fifth, we like to be unobserved. Sometimes we feel happier when nobody can see or hear what we are doing, or what we are doing in a group of consenting and like-minded people.

This is not a complete list of private matters. Nor is it a list that is independent of cultures. Much to do with privacy, and to what extent we are comfortable with doing things in public and how much we mind others knowing about us, is a result of our upbringing and our society's norms. This last point is not without relevance. It may be that there are cases in which instead of insisting on or demanding privacy, it would be more important to try to change some of society's values.

Why Is Privacy Good?

There are various reasons why we want or do not want personal details revealed, to be seen doing certain things, and so on. The reasons vary depending on the type of privacy. Sometimes it is embarrassment. If someone sees me performing some bodily function normally performed in private, no harm comes to me except perhaps embarrassment. I just do not like being seen doing this. Or it might be embarrassment about some aspect of my past being exposed; something about which I feel shame. At other times we value privacy because of harm or potential harm resulting from disclosure of certain information. I may lose my job or not get one that I want if something about my past is disclosed. The more that others know about me, particularly those with power, the less control I have over my own life. If I am in business, I may lose some competitive advantage if various aspects of my activities become known. Sometimes the value of privacy lies in the development of a friendship that is not possible or much more difficult if we can never be alone with that person. The presence of a third party can often be inhibiting. At other times we value privacy because we need time to think or carry out some activity like writing, which demands careful thought. While it may not be impossible to do this with company, it will frequently be much more difficult to concentrate.

It might be argued that none of what has been said shows that privacy is a good thing in itself. All of the problems caused by a lack or an invasion of privacy occur only as a result of our conditioning or because of what others do with what they discover about us. I get embarrassed only because certain things are done only in private in our society, but I could get used to doing them in public. Plenty of people in other cultures have. I could learn to think and write in public, and develop deep friendships with others around. And there is nothing harmful in others discovering anything about me if they do not use it against me. All of this is probably true, but not really to the point, given the sort of society in which we find ourselves. In a different society privacy may not be important, but in one like ours it does have value. There are undoubtedly cases in which it would be better to try to change attitudes or practices than to place great emphasis on privacy, but that does not mean that it does not have value to us now.

We have looked at some specific reasons why we value privacy. Is there any general moral principle from which the right to privacy follows? Perhaps the most obvious is the utilitarian one. Lack of privacy or invasion of privacy can harm individuals, although of course they do not do so necessarily. Sometimes it is merely a nuisance, and sometimes we do not care at all. Nevertheless, privacy does or can protect individuals from various kinds of harm, and therefore is to be valued. Another reason for privacy might be respect for persons. If we respect people we treat them as ends in themselves, and not purely as means to some end. Employees, for example, should be treated as persons who have value in themselves, and not just as units who can produce. If people are respected they will not be treated as merely *things*, and therefore not as things to be observed as we might observe sparrows or computers. Invasion of privacy, certainly in many cases, involves treating the observed as means and not as ends. They are things to be "looked at" for some other end, and not people to be respected.

Freedom and Privacy

Privacy protects some freedoms and restricts others. It protects an individual's freedom to be alone, to do things without others intruding, and to control what others know about him or her. However, it restricts the extent to which an individual can observe others and what he or she can learn about others. More importantly, it restricts the freedom of the state or other powerful institutions to control individuals. It might in fact be argued that the moral value of privacy comes from its specific function in promoting the liberty of individuals by restricting the scope of the power of the state and others in positions of strength.

PRIVACY AND INFORMATION TECHNOLOGY

The issue of privacy rears its head in a number of areas related to information technology. Here we will consider three: personal data, hacking, and surveillance.

Personal Data

It was revealed in the *Sunday Times* that one of Britain's largest banks kept records of customers' political opinions, and that other companies kept records of sexual behaviour (Hadfield and Skipworth 1993b). This raises the question of what information businesses, governments, or other bodies should be allowed to keep on file about customers, employees, citizens, or anyone else. This question has become much more urgent in recent times, with the advent of computer-based databases and technology for the automatic collection of information. These databases can hold vast amounts of information that can also be accessed quickly and cheaply. Therefore, to a much greater extent than ever before, there is the capacity to store, collect, and access information on individuals that can be used for many purposes. The ACM recognises this problem:

> Computing and communication technology enables the collection and exchange of personal information on a scale unprecedented in the history of civilization. Thus there is increased potential for violating the privacy of individuals and groups. It is the responsibility of professionals to maintain the privacy and integrity of data describing individuals. (ACM 1992: 1.7)

There are really two issues here: what may be stored, and what should be done with it. First, what is wrong with storing personal data? In many cases, nothing. Health records must be kept by doctors and hospitals, education records by schools and universities, borrower records by libraries, and financial records by banks. In all of these cases the individuals whose data it is benefit by such storage. But even here only what is necessary should be stored, and then only for as long as it is required. The ACM statement goes into some detail on this:

> This imperative [the responsibility of professionals to maintain the privacy and integrity of data] implies that only the necessary amount of personal information be collected in a system, that retention and disposal periods for that information be clearly defined and enforced, and that personal information gathered for a specific purpose not be used for other purposes without consent of the individual(s). These principles apply to electronic communications, including electronic mail, and prohibit procedures that capture or monitor electronic user data, including messages, without the permission of users or bona fide authorization related to system operation and maintenance. User data observed during the normal duties of system operation and maintenance must be treated with strictest confidentiality. (ACM 1992: 1.7)

The first points in this statement mention policy matters. Governments, corporations, professional bodies, and so on should have policies spelt out that state explicitly what information is collected and stored, for how long, for what purpose, and the like. The latter points are directed specifically at professionals who work with computers and who have access to the material, but access because of their technological expertise and not because of any necessity to use the information.

One professional group that has long been interested in privacy issues—since well before the introduction of computer technology—is the library profession. The ALA puts its concern this way:

> The ethical responsibilities of librarians, as well as statutes in most states and the District of Columbia, protect the privacy of library users. Confidentiality extends to "information sought or received, and materials consulted, borrowed, acquired," and includes database search records, reference interviews, circulation records, interlibrary loan records, and other personally identifiable uses of library materials, facilities, or services. (ALA 1996: 52.4)

Why are librarians so concerned about privacy? The reading habits of library users are the business of nobody except the user, but that in itself is not too important. My preference for unsugared, black coffee rather than the sweet, white variety is also the business of nobody but me and any person making my coffee, but worrying about the privacy of this information seems a bit extreme. While much information about users that is stored in library databases might not be much more important than my preference in coffee, in general, reading habits do reveal a little more about a person. It has been argued that what someone reads is very close to what he or she thinks, and therefore the ability to discover what is read is, in effect, the ability to find out what is thought. This latter ability then facilitates thought control (Million and Fisher 1986: 349). This is a bit strong. While someone might be able to get a pretty good idea of what we think on various issues by an examination of our total reading pattern, any particular item will not reveal much. Our purpose in reading an item would need to be known. Reading something in order to criticise it is very different from reading something to get support for a particular point of view. And even if a great deal is revealed about the way we think by looking at reading patterns, there is still a big jump to "thought control," whatever that is.

Nevertheless, it is not difficult to imagine situations in which governments, advertising agencies, or other groups could make use of this information for purposes not beneficial to the individual. For example, according to Angela Million and Kim Fisher, in the United States the Moral Majority organization attempted to obtain the names of school districts and individuals who had borrowed a film on sexual maturity from the Washington State Library (1986: 346). Sometimes of course this type of information might be beneficial to the community, for example when law enforcement agencies need information for criminal investigations. The ALA notes this too, but makes no concessions. The library records are still to remain private and released only at the direction of the courts.

The American Library Association recognizes that law enforcement agencies and officers may occasionally believe that library records contain information which may be helpful to the
investigation of criminal activity. If there is a reasonable basis
to believe such records are necessary to the progress of an investigation or prosecution, the American judicial system provides the mechanism for seeking release of such confidential
records: the issuance of a court order, following a showing of
good cause based on specific facts, by a court of competent ju-
risdiction. (ALA 1996: 52.4)

Is this hard line taken by the ALA justified? Confidentiality and privacy
are valued highly by some professions, such as clergy and medical practitioners. In both cases it is argued that breaking the confidentiality under
any circumstances would lead to lack of trust, which in turn would make
people less willing to seek help, often much-needed, from these quarters.
So in areas like this it is plausible to argue that the privacy of individuals
should be placed above the needs of the community, even law enforcement agencies. In fact, the argument would probably be that the community is served better, in the long term anyway, with this confidentiality
intact. Librarians can hardly make such a strong case. The library's operation, and the reader's potential benefits from using it, do not depend to
any great extent on trust, certainly not in the way that the clergy and the
medical profession depend on trust. However, borrowers can be harmed
if their records are not kept private. The burden of proof should be on
those who want records made public, or at least available. The privacy of
the individual can be overridden, but only for the public good, and not
merely to serve the curiosity or profit of other individuals.

So much for libraries; what about other organisations or businesses?
Suppose that a supermarket created a database of all purchases by customers. This could be done easily and automatically when the customers
paid by credit card. The information gathered could be used to target advertising perhaps. But even if this type of data has benefit for the supermarket, it is dubious whether it ought to be collected. It is difficult to see
of what benefit it could be to the individual customer, but it is not so difficult to see potential harm, particularly if it is sold or otherwise made
available to other parties. An insurance company, for example, might decide that a potential customer buys too much food with a high fat content,
and consider him not to be a good risk. We will consider who owns this
data and has a right to sell it, and then look more closely at the use made
of this data, and in particular at data matching.

Who does own personal data? In the supermarket case perhaps it is the
supermarket. The store owners spent time and money collecting it and it
is stored on their equipment, but is it really theirs to store and collect? It is,

after all, information about particular individuals, about us. If we consent to the collection and storage, then their claim is more legitimate. But what is consent here? If we know that it is being collected, know what it will be used for, and have a genuine choice of buying at another store where no personal data is collected, then perhaps the supermarket does own the data. But if we do not know of the collection, or its purpose, or we cannot choose to patronise a store that does not collect data, either because there is no other store close enough or because all stores collect data, then the supermarket's ownership claims are dubious. It is not clear that we have consented in any real way.

Why is the collection of personal data without informed consent illegitimate? The situation here is quite different from that in a library where borrowing records are kept. Libraries cannot function for very long without keeping a record of who has borrowed what. A supermarket, on the other hand, has no need to know what individuals buy. It can function quite well just knowing how much of what is sold. Collecting personal data about someone without their consent amounts to treating that person as merely an object and not as a person deserving of respect, and is almost certainly an invasion of privacy. The collector then can no more claim ownership of the data than can a thief claim ownership of the goods he has stolen. The data is therefore not the collector's to sell or make available to others. Suppose that the data is collected with the full and informed consent of the individuals involved. Even here it does not follow that the owner has the moral right to make it available to others without the further consent of the individuals whose personal data are involved. Doing so makes personal data into just another commodity, and this is wrong for two reasons: The potential harm to the individuals, and the scant respect it shows for them as persons.

There are two main reasons for the dangers to the individual of using personal data, particularly outside the context in which it was collected, even if all those using it are people of good will. One reason is that context is important, and the other is that human life is fuzzy while computer systems are precise. First, facts out of context can be misleading. Actually they make little sense at all—witness the silliness of Gradgrind and his emphasis on teaching facts (especially his views on Sissy Jupe's inability to define a horse) in *Hard Times* (Dickens 1854: 3). The fact that I buy foods high in fats on its own means nothing except that I buy foods high in fats. I might be regularly buying them for someone else, so it would be blatantly unfair for an insurance company to use this information in assessing my suitability as a customer. The company would not be working with false data, but it would be making false inferences from the data. Second, human life is not precise, and this is a major problem with the practice of matching data in different databases. The problem is that we work with imprecise notions and boundaries, our languages are imprecise, we forget what we have done, and we often do not see relationships and implications. Computer systems, on the other hand, are precise; hence if they are superimposed on ordinary human life they will almost certainly show all sorts of inconsistencies and so on even in the case of well-intentioned and honest people.

Hacking

There have been some dramatic instances of hacking that have led to considerable public outcry. Consider, for example, the following:

> European Cancer Research, Luxembourg. System hacked, had to be removed. Result: couldn't operate on a 10-year-old boy for six days. European Weather Forecasting, Bracknell, Berkshire. Forecasting service for ships at sea. March 1991, Bay of Biscay. Weather forecasting satellite not working—integrity broken by hackers. Ship lost at sea. . . . Turin University. AIDS research results changed. Now unreliable. . . . Pap smear tests, conducted in England. Women were told they'd tested positive. In fact the results were wrong—someone had broken in and changed them. (Bass 1995: 40)

These cases of hacking make it look obvious that hacking is morally wrong and ought to be condemned. But most incidents are not as dramatic as these, and often hacking is not looked upon as being very serious. Sometimes it is even defended and praised.

It must be noted before proceeding that the word "hacking" has a number of uses. In one innocuous sense, a hacker is just a person who likes sitting at a terminal, programming the computer (usually without properly planning the program beforehand), or otherwise delving into a system's capabilities. In the sense used in this book, a hacker is someone who uses his or her computing skills to gain access to computer systems or areas of systems for which they have no authorisation (see Forester and Morrison 1995: 77–79 for various uses of "hacking"). In this sense, hacking may be seen as being related to privacy and to property. It is related to privacy in that, at least in some cases, it is an invasion of privacy. It is related to property in that it is a kind of trespass.

What is wrong with hacking? If it is wrong, it is because of what is wrong with invasion of privacy and trespass. We will look at trespass first. Trespass is the entering of territory that you have no right to enter because it belongs to or is legitimately controlled by another. Several issues are raised here too. One is the notion of trespass as such, which relies on the assumption that some individual or body may legitimately stop someone else from entering some area, be it geographical, as is normally the case, or logical, as is the case in computing. The other issue is this: even if it could be established that people have a right to go anywhere (either geographically or logically), should they be allowed to change the state of what they find or freely report what they discover?

Why is trespassing wrong? If I walk through a privately owned field and do nothing except walk, and report nothing of what I see, I harm nobody. This is much like flying over the field in an airplane, which is not trespass (unless I am flying very, very low!). It could be argued that this trespass (that is, walking in the field) is an invasion of the owner's privacy, in the sense that his or her space is being invaded. This has some force, although it has much more if we are talking about someone's house or office. What does seem to be true is that trespass is not morally wrong in itself. It is only wrong insofar as harm is caused or privacy is invaded.

What if the hacker does no harm and all that he does is look? As we saw earlier, we value privacy for a variety of reasons. One is that there is more potential for harm the more that is known about us. The hacker may not use the information gained, but we cannot be sure of that. This leads to an even more important problem. If it is known that someone has hacked his way into some system, the integrity of the data is under a cloud. Has it been tampered with or not? Changes made to digitally stored data are not easily detectable.

It has been suggested that hacking can be beneficial (Forester and Morrison 1995: chapter 4). The possibility of hacking allows some protection against powerful states or corporations. The more information that is kept about us, the greater the potential for control over our lives. Hackers challenge this concept of all-powerful states and corporations. Another argument is that if systems are not secure, there is nothing wrong with entering them. The first of these defences has force only if hackers are largely benign. But this may well not be the case, as the earlier examples show. The second defence has no weight. If I leave my door open this is not a general invitation for anyone at all to enter, nor is the fact that I do not have a high electrified fence around my property.

Surveillance

Employers clearly have some rights in seeing that their employees are working satisfactorily. It is not only in the employer's interests that the required tasks are performed efficiently and well, but it may also be in the interests of other employees and the general public. As employees we do not want to support, at our expense, lazy or incompetent colleagues. As consumers we do not want to buy overpriced and substandard goods and services. But that does not mean that "anything goes" when it comes to employee monitoring or surveillance. Unfortunately, some may say fortunately, the widespread use of computers has made workplace surveillance very easy. Keystrokes can be monitored, the work on your screen may be brought up on the screen of another, and of course telephones can be bugged and listening devices installed to listen in on the informal conversations of employees. Common software for accessing the Internet logs all activity, so that a record is kept of all visits to all sites. A supervisor can easily find who did what on the Internet!

Does this monitoring matter? It is often defended by employers, who argue that it is in the interests of all. Employees who are not performing well are weeded out. Those doing their jobs well can be rewarded on objective criteria. In addition, and probably most importantly, it leads to more efficient and profitable businesses. But there are other important things in life besides efficiency and profitability. Should employees be under surveillance every minute of the working day? Or, which is much the same, should they be in a situation in which every minute of the working day they suspect that they might be under surveillance? Or, should there be surveillance about which they know nothing? These would seem to be unjustified invasions of privacy. An employer might argue that while the employees are at work they are being paid and so their time belongs to the employer. Moreover, they are using the employer's facilities. But employees are humans, not machines. Humans (even employers) must make decisions, some of which will be the wrong ones, and we frequently make other mistakes. This is just part of being human. We get tired, bored, frustrated, angry, lose concentration, and so on. It is therefore blatantly unfair to monitor people constantly or in a manner in which they are constantly aware that they might be under surveillance. It is undoubtedly an unjustified invasion of privacy. It is highly likely to harm those watched, by increasing stress and lowering morale (Nussbaum: 1989), and it is certainly not showing them any respect as persons.

Another form of monitoring, perhaps more benign but often discussed, is that of monitoring employees' E-mail. While this might be thought to be akin to opening private mail or listening in to private conversations, the argument is that because the system on which the E-mail operates is owned by the employers, they have a right to read any messages. But do they? The fact that two people are conversing in my house does not give me an automatic right to listen to what they are saying. But what if the two people are my employees? This makes no difference. All I am paying for is their labour. What they say to customers might be my business, but what they say to each other is not. Perhaps the cases are not analogous, because in the E-mail case they are using my equipment, while in the other they are not. But what they say is still none of my business. The fact that they are saying anything might be my business if they are wearing out the equipment or hindering the work of others or themselves. Banning or limiting private conversations might be justified, but monitoring them is not. Perhaps this still misses the point. How will I know if the

E-mail is being used for private discussions if I do not monitor it? I will not know unless I am told, but if no problems are being caused by overuse and so on, there is no need to worry. If there are problems such as the overloading of the system, some steps may need to be taken, but even here actually reading messages would rarely be necessary. There could be a limit put on the length of messages or the number sent. Employing people does not confer the right to monitor their private conversations or the right to stop them from having such conversations.

There does, of course, need to be some balance between the rights of individuals and the rights of the group as a whole. However, in the case of electronic monitoring, it is difficult to see where it might be justified in the workplace. The harm or potential harm to employees is just too great. It could be justified in the interests of national security or to fight fairly serious crime, cases in which the individuals or state are likely to be seriously harmed. But a mere increase in profit is no adequate justification.

SUMMARY

Privacy does cause concern in the computer age, although we saw that when we think about it carefully, it is not quite so clear just what the worry is. Privacy, like freedom and property, is more easily spoken about loosely than carefully. While not attempting to find a definition, we did try to see what is commonly meant by people when they talk of, or are worried about, privacy. We then attempted to see why privacy is usually thought to be such a good thing. Finally, we looked more specifically at privacy in relation to personal data, hacking, and employee surveillance.

REFERENCES

ACM Code of Ethics and Professional Conduct. 1992. [On-line]. Available gopher://
ACM.ORG:70/00%5Bthe_files.constitution%5Dbylaw17.txt

ALA Policy Manual, Section Two (Position and Public Policy Statements). 1996. 52.4
Confidentiality of Library Records. [On-line]. Available gopher://gopher.
ala.org:70/11/alagophviii

ACS Code of Ethics. 1993. In electronic format. *IT Practitioner's Handbook.* Darling-
hurst, NSW: Australian Computer Society.

Bass, Jeremy. 1995. In the belly of the beast. *Information Age* [Melbourne, Australia]
1 (September): 36–40.

Dickens, Charles. 1854. *Hard Times*; page citation to edition of Ford and Monod, 1966.

Forester, Tom, and Perry Morrison. 1995. *Computer Ethics: Cautionary Tales and
Ethical Dilemmas in Computing.* 2d ed. Cambridge, MA: MIT Press.

Hadfield, Greg, and Mark Skipworth. 1993a. Private lives for sale in illicit info-
market. *Sunday Times* (London), 18 July.

Hadfield, Greg, and Mark Skipworth. 1993b. Firms keep "dirty data" on sex lives
of staff. *Sunday Times* (London), 25 July.

McIntosh, Trudi. 1995. Privacy issue to dominate '90s. *The Australian*, 14 March.

Million, Angela C., and Kim N. Fisher. 1986. Library records: A review of confidentiality laws and policies. *Journal of Academic Librarianship* 11: 346–49.

Nussbaum, Karen. 1991. Computer monitoring: A threat to the right to privacy? In *Ethical Issues in Information Systems*, ed. Roy Dejoie, George Fowler, and David Paradice. Boston: Boyd & Fraser, 134–39.

FURTHER READING

Anderson, A. J. 1989. The FBI wants you—to spy. *Library Journal* (June 15): 37–39.

Benn, Stanley I. 1988. *A Theory of Freedom*. Cambridge: Cambridge University Press, chapters 14, 15.

Dejoie, Roy, George Fowler, and David Paradice. 1991. *Ethical Issues in Information Systems*. Boston: Boyd & Fraser, chapter 3.

MacNeil, Heather. 1992. *Without Consent: The Ethics of Disclosing Personal Information in Public Archives*. Metuchen, NJ: The Scarecrow Press.

Miller, Seumas. 1996. Privacy, databases and computers. *Australian Library Review* 13 (February): 60–64.

Pennock, J., and J. Chapman, eds. 1971. *Nomos XIII: Privacy*. New York: Atherton Press.

7

Responsibility

In the twentieth century B.C. the Code of Hammurabi declared that if a house collapsed and killed its owner, the builder of the house was to be put to death. In the twentieth century A.D. many builders of computer software would deny responsibility and pass the "entire risk" to the user. (Nissenbaum 1994: 79)

In this chapter and the next, the emphasis shifts a little, away from information as a passive resource, to issues related to information generated by computers; to software that *does* something.

Workers in the computing and information fields have special responsibilities by virtue of their expertise. People trust experts in the area of their expertise, and that trust is broken if the expert is careless, incompetent, or intentionally gives false or misleading advice. So experts have a responsibility to be careful, competent, and honest in their work. It might be argued of course that every person has this responsibility, and in addition, that we all should always be careful and honest. What makes the expert's responsibility special is the sense in which the word "responsible" is used in this context.

The word "responsible" has two importantly distinct senses. First, there is the *causal* sense: We may say that Jack was responsible for a death, or that lightning was responsible for a fire, meaning that Jack caused the death or that lightning caused the fire. Secondly, there is the *accountability* sense, concerning who should be held accountable for something, whose moral account, as it were, should be credited if the thing is good or debited if it is bad; who should be praised or rewarded if it is good or blamed or punished if it is bad. In this sense we would not normally hold the lightning responsible for the fire (though some might hold a god such as Thor responsible for sending it), and we may not even hold Jack responsible for the death; he caused it, we might say, but he is not responsible because he is only three years old, or insane, or could not have been expected to foresee the consequences of his action on that occasion. The two senses often come together in that a person who is responsible for something in the causal sense is often held responsible for it in the accountability sense, but it is important to note the difference. For the discussion of the expert's responsibility, the second and stronger sense is the central one. Experts are, or ought to be, accountable for their actions in their professional fields.

It is interesting to note the lack of emphasis on responsibility in this sense in the various codes of ethics mentioned in this book. The ACM code is the strongest, speaking of "the obligation to accept personal accountability for professional work" (1992: 2.6). But it says this in the context of requesting a change in an assignment and not directly with respect to work carried out, and it follows that statement with "On some occasions other ethical principles may take greater priority." Nothing is said about what those other principles might be. The ACS has just one short statement, "I will accept responsibility for my work" (1993: 2.5). The ALA does not explicitly mention accountability for malpractice in either its *Code of Ethics* or its *Policy Manual*.

The emphasis in this chapter is on responsibility and accountability for computer software failures. The issues of responsibility and accountability arise in many other contexts too, of course, for computer and information professionals. There is the responsibility, for example, for giving correct or the best available information. This is probably the area concerning accountability most discussed by librarians (see Katz 1992: 226–28). However, the introduction of computer technology raises no new issues here, and it is these new issues that are of central concern in this book.

When people talk about responsibility for software failures, for example, they usually have the accountability sense in mind (see Nissenbaum 1994), and accordingly we shall focus on that sense in this chapter. First we must consider the circumstances under which someone or some group should be held accountable for some event. Then we shall look at questions relating to software. Is it inherently flawed, and why? Under what circumstances should it be released? Finally, and most importantly, who, if anyone, is accountable for software failures?

ACCOUNTABILITY

You are sitting in a plane about ten kilometres above the surface of the earth, and the fly-by-wire system fails due to some software fault. You are writing a letter, and on the eighth page the word processing package "falls over"; you have forgotten to save your work. You read an electronic text on mushrooms that contains some false information on the safety of a particular mushroom; you eat it with disastrous consequences. You manage your vineyard with the help of an expert system that advises against spraying; you take the advice and lose most of your crop. In the first two cases the software is at fault. It contains some "bug." In the third case the fault is with the information. It may be a mistake in the sense that the author meant to classify that mushroom as poisonous but for some reason did not, or it might be that at the time it was believed to be edible. In the final case the problem might be that there is some bug in the program, or it might reflect the inadequate knowledge that was built into the system. Our primary concern is with software faults, not with incorrect information. As important as that topic is, there are not really any issues in faulty electronic information that are not the same as those in any other medium. In which of these cases of software failure, if any, is someone accountable? And who is accountable? Can we make sense of the notion of accountability at all if a group is responsible for the software, as will normally be the case? Does the fact that all software of any complexity will contain errors make a difference? If all software is inevitably going to be faulty to some extent, when is "good enough" good enough, that is, when should software be released? We will examine these and other issues in what follows.

When Is One Accountable?

When is person P accountable for some event E? At least three conditions must be satisfied: (1) P must have caused E, or knowingly allowed E to happen when he or she could have prevented it; (2) P must have intended to cause E, or allowed it through neglect or carelessness; (3) P must have been free to choose to do or not to do whatever caused E. Condition (1) just says that P must have done whatever it was that caused E or not done what could have prevented it. This is satisfied if I drown someone or if I allow someone to drown when I could easily have rescued him or her. The second condition shows the importance of intention. If I come across two drowning people in a situation in which it is physically possible for me to rescue only one of them, I have played a causal role in the drowning of one of them when I rescue the other. But I would certainly have had no intention to be a cause of the drowning, so I can hardly be held accountable. Condition (3) shows that the situation is similar if I have no choice. If I watch someone drown while I, against my will, am tied to a tree, I certainly do not do anything to prevent the drowning, but I have no choice in the matter.

Collective Accountability

Many people are involved in the design, development, sale, and use of a typical computer system. Therefore when something goes wrong, it is not always easy to say who is accountable, and who, if anyone, ought to be liable for any damages. We will first look at the general question of whether it makes sense to hold a group accountable for some event. In everyday talk we do this frequently. Germany is blamed for the invasion of Poland, Iraq for that of Kuwait, and the United States for the Vietnam War. Australia is held accountable for the plight of its indigenous people and France for any possible effects of nuclear tests in the Pacific. Companies are sued for oil spills and the release of dangerous drugs, and sporting teams for unruly behaviour on airplanes.

Exactly who or what is held accountable in these cases? Not everyone in Germany or Iraq can be held accountable for the invasions, nor can all Americans, Australians, or French, or all members of companies or sporting teams for problems caused by their particular group's behaviour. Certainly not all the individuals are at fault, and those who are, are not all equally so. There is, however, a sense in which all, with only several exceptions, can plausibly be held accountable. If I do nothing to try to change the situation of my country's indigenous people or try to stop my company's carelessness, I am helping to perpetuate a climate in which actions like those mentioned above can occur. So I can and ought to be held accountable to some extent, even though I did not cause the events or intend them to happen. The exceptions are those in which I have protested or attempted to change the situation, or I am not in a position in which I could do anything, or if I could not reasonably be expected to know of the situation (see Feinberg 1970: chapter 9 for more discussion). In other words, it is reasonable in general to attribute accountability to organised groups and also to individuals because of the group to which they belong. If a computer system fails then, it is reasonable to hold some group accountable for the failure. If the members of a group, even if not all of them, satisfy the conditions for accountability specified earlier, then the group can be held accountable.

SOFTWARE RELIABILITY

It is generally accepted, at least in computing circles, that software is inherently flawed. This might be one motive for calling program errors "bugs," as if they just occur and are the fault of nobody. We will return to this "bug talk" later, and now consider why there might be this problem with software.

Is Software Inherently Flawed?

Software is not inherently flawed if by "flawed" it is meant that it is impossible in principle to develop software that is error-free. What is meant is that *in practice* it is impossible to remove all errors from any reasonably complex system. This could of course be just an excuse for slovenliness, so we need to see why it is claimed to be so hard to rid programs of errors. Why is this more difficult than in the case of other products?

Several reasons have been advanced to support the case that software development has some unique problems. First there is the complexity of software systems. Any reasonably sized program is going to contain a large number of statements (like "IF" or "CASE") that determine which section of code will be executed, and many variables whose values keep changing. Understanding a program written by others is no easy task, hence the emphasis on good, clear documentation and program structure. One of the motivations for the continual search for new and better programming paradigms is the understandability of programs. The easier a program is to understand the easier it is to maintain and the more easily one may reuse code and adapt it for new programs. This leads to more efficient software development, fewer bugs, and less expensive systems (or higher profits!). The "spaghetti code" of the early days of programming was found to be much too difficult to understand. Structured programming methods were developed to make programming simpler and programs more reliable and understandable, and the recent, and still current, surge in interest in Object Oriented techniques is a further step in the same direction (or so it is hoped). A strength of the Object Oriented approach, it is claimed, is that it corresponds more closely with everyday thinking in which we tend to work with objects and the relationships between them. The closer the programming paradigm is to our normal thinking patterns, the easier programs should be to develop and to understand, and so it ought to be easier to make them more reliable.

A second problem, following from the first, is the difficulty of thoroughly testing a program of any complexity. Testing all possible combinations of input values would be a practical impossibility in many cases. Testing all plausible combinations, even when practical, leaves open the possibility that when in use, the program may encounter unexpected input values that may not have been tested. So while meticulous testing is vital, in any particular instance it is unlikely that all errors will be eliminated. An example of the problem, admittedly an extreme one, concerns the U.S. requirement that in civilian aircraft, the probability of certain catastrophic failures in air traffic control systems must be no worse than 10^{-9} per hour. To establish this level of reliability in software, it has been estimated that the program would need to be executed continuously for about 100,000 years (Littlewood and Strigini 1992: 40).

A third problem has to do with the very nature of digital computers. A digital computer is in one discrete state or in another, with no intermediate position. A memory location has either the value 1 or 0—either the state is the correct one or it is a wrong one. It cannot be partly correct. So software may not give any indication that it is about to fail in the way that a car might. In the case of a car, often small problems become noticeable without causing much inconvenience. They gradually increase until, if they are not remedied, the car becomes dangerous or undriveable. Software does not degrade gracefully and gradually like this and it does not wear out. There may be no sign that something is wrong. It will normally work perfectly or intolerably. (This is an overstatement. Programs can have bugs that are no more than annoying. But the important point is that these problems are not normally signs of greater problems to come.) This makes both testing and predicting problems more difficult. (For more discussion see Parnas et al. 1990)

"Bugs"

While it is probably true that programs will inevitably contain errors, there is a danger in calling these errors "bugs." This gives the impression that they just occur, without human intervention as it were. While this was true of the first bug (a moth found by Grace Murray Hopper in the Mark I computer in the 1940s) (Kurzweil 1990: 178–79), it is not true of program errors. They are the result of human mistakes and should be looked at in this light. Christ said, "Woe to the world because of offences! for it must be that offences come; but woe to that man by whom the offence cometh!" (Matt. 18:7) Paraphrasing this, we should look on program errors thus; "Woe to programs, because of errors, for it is inevitable that they will have errors; but woe to that programmer by whom the error cometh!"

When Should Software Be Released?

In the best of all possible worlds, software would be released only when it was free of errors. But this is not the best of all possible worlds, not with respect to software anyway. There can be no guarantee that it will be error-free. Therefore judgements need to be made about when it should be released, when it is "good enough," and perhaps if it should be released at all. The answers given here will have implications for the question of who is accountable if or when some problem occurs.

There are several main groups of software players (see Collins et al. 1994). There are the *developers* who develop and sell the software; the *buyers* who buy and own a copy; the *users* who use the system; and finally the *penumbra*, comprising anyone affected by the use of the software. These groups are not necessarily distinct. For example, the same person might be the user and the buyer, and perhaps in isolated cases also the developer. And any of the first three groups may of course overlap with the penumbra. But drawing these distinctions in roles does make it easier to discuss the issues of release time and accountability.

An obvious point is that the release of software should not make a situation worse than it was without the software. This is clearly the case with software used in high-risk situations, such as civilian aircraft fly-by-wire systems. Increasing the risk of a plane crash seems a bit silly, but we will say a little more about these critical systems later and for the moment look at less life-threatening ones. While it may seem obvious that software should not make a situation worse, it is perhaps not so obvious just what this means. Worse for whom? This is one place in which the role distinctions drawn above come in useful. Early release may benefit some, such as the developers and the buyers, but it may make life less easy for the users if they are required to work with a product that is prone to "falling over" due to program errors. Other software may be beneficial to all groups except the penumbra. It might be claimed that in a capitalist system this would not happen because it is not in a business' interests to sell or use a shoddy product. This of course is a myth. Shoddy products can be very profitable in the short term or if there is collusion between businesses.

Software, like most tools and technologies, is designed to make life better in some way. This does not always eventuate, but it is normally the intention. So the main criterion in the release of software is whether or not there are benefits that outweigh costs. But benefits for whom? Clearly the developer wants to maximise profits and the buyer wants a product as good and as inexpensive as possible. But these should be considerations only if the users and, more importantly, the penumbra are not worse off. Of the four groups, the penumbra are the least powerful. They have no control over what software is used, or for what purpose. They are purely beneficiaries or victims of the system, so their interests should have great importance. The users in many cases will be in a similar position, though normally with a little more influence. If the penumbra benefit, or are not harmed, then the main concern should be the interests of the users. It is only if neither of these two groups is likely to be harmed by error-prone software that it is justifiable to release it. The reason for arguing this way is that both the developers and the buyers have control over their own destinies in this case. If developers suffer a loss due to the release of error-prone software, it is largely their own fault. And if buyers purchase a product that is not ready, provided that they know of the problems, they too must be prepared to accept responsibility for their own actions in purchasing it.

Suppose that a new word processing package is released that contains many new features but also some annoying problems such as occasionally "hanging" without saving. It might well be that the users are happy enough with this new product because it is so much better than any alternatives, even though they must frequently save their work and perhaps waste time in rebooting their machines more often than they would like.

In this situation release of faulty software is justified, provided of course that no deceit is involved. The situation is a bit different in life-threatening cases. Not too many people would be happy if the software on an airplane was as error-prone as their new word processor or operating system! We might even be tempted to argue that such software should not be used at all unless it can be guaranteed to be error-free, in which case we would in effect be arguing that it should not be used at all. This line of argument is only plausible of course if in these life-threatening cases planes are safer without the software than with it. And it is not obvious that this is so. It may be that planes flying with the aid of software, even though it does contain some errors, are still safer than those without it. So if the risks to passengers, the main penumbra here, are lessened, then the release and use of software is justifiable.

ACCOUNTABILITY FOR SOFTWARE FAILURE

If it is inevitable that sometimes software will fail, is it reasonable to hold anyone accountable? In a sense it is nobody's fault. Nobody is free to produce error-free software, and so condition (3) for accountability, that is that one must have been free to choose, seems to be impossible to satisfy. But it is not quite like this. While it may not be possible in practice to develop software free from errors, it does not follow that any particular error could not have been avoided with a little more care. Therefore, for any particular software failure, it is possible that someone could have fixed the error that caused it.

We look now at a fairly undramatic case. Suppose that some business has purchased a financial package to help bill its customers each month. Unfortunately, periodically the package puts the wrong amount on the bill, sometimes overcharging and sometimes undercharging. While this is not life- or business-threatening, it is an annoyance, particularly to the users and the customers. Who, if anyone, is accountable for this situation? The most obvious person (or group) to blame is the developer. The developer caused the problem, allowed it to happen through neglect or carelessness, and could have avoided it. So the three conditions for accountability have been met—the developer is accountable. However, it is not quite so straightforward. The developer might claim, justifiably, that the buyer knew that the product contained, or probably contained, errors. It is, after all, well known that all or most software does have errors, and as a result developers normally refuse to guarantee their products. The buyer, if informed of the software's inherent unreliability or that the developer will not guarantee it, must also accept responsibility. And the buyer can hardly claim ignorance. Software is rarely guaranteed. Rather, there are disclaimers. A typical example is this:

> The Licensed Software is provided "as is." All warranties and representations of any kind with regard to the Licensed Software are hereby disclaimed, including the implied warranties of merchantability and fitness for a particular purpose. Under no circumstances will the manufacturer or developer of the Licensed Software be liable for any consequential, incidental, special, or exemplary damages, even if appraised of the likelihood of such damages occurring. (Information Builders Inc., *Level 5 Object*)

It could quite plausibly be argued that buyers who are willing to accept this sort of disclaimer are also accountable for any damage caused by the software malfunction. They, after all, are the ones who bought it in the full knowledge that the developers cannot and are not willing to verify its reliability.

Are the users also accountable? Unless they are the same person or people as the buyers, they are not accountable except when they can influence the buyers of the software. They are victims to a large extent, as are the customers, the penumbra.

It was argued earlier that in order to be accountable, the three conditions discussed at the beginning of this chapter must be satisfied. We saw that the developers do satisfy them, but the buyers do not seem to. So how can they be accountable? When they buy the software in the knowledge that it contains errors, they are also acquiring some of the accountability. Accountability goes with informed ownership. Most people, apart from the owners of the copyright on software, seem to accept this. If my dog attacks someone, I am accountable. If buyers are accountable, does that release the developers from accountability? It would seem to depend on the extent to which the developers explained the possible and probable problems to the buyers. If there is any deceit on the part of the developers, then they must remain primarily accountable. However, if the buyers are fully informed of the risks, most of the accountability resides there.

We have argued that both developers and buyers can be accountable for software faults, and perhaps jointly. Our argument was based on the fact that developers satisfy all of the conditions for accountability, and the fact that accountability goes with informed ownership, other things being equal. Deborah Johnson and John Mulvey (1995) look at the problem in a different way. They argue that accountability presumes a set of norms, and that someone is accountable only if they act outside those norms. Therefore, in order for accountability to be attributed in the software case, the norms of behaviour for software developers (systems designers in their terms) must be carefully enunciated. If there is no *normal* behaviour we cannot tell whether anything outside the norm was done, and so we cannot tell if the developers are responsible or accountable. They see these norms as linked with the professionalisation of systems design, and argue that the developers themselves should clearly articulate them. "Articulation of norms of behavior in the field will shape the expectations of clients and third parties. It will move the field in the direction of professionalization, creating a form of accountability that, in turn, will promote public trust in computer decision systems" (Johnson and Mulvey 1995: 64).

What is valuable about this way of looking at the problem is that it gives some fairly objective way of seeing whether or not a developer could reasonably be held accountable in a particular case. The weakness is that it is only as good as the norms. If the accepted standards of behaviour are too low, some developers might observe them but still justifiably be held accountable for a problem. Norms or standard practices are normally minimum standards for behaviour, and there are times when we would expect a "professional" to operate at a higher level than that.

Why is this question of accountability so important? When there is accountability there is more care. And given the increasing reliance on software, more care in its development is certainly required. If developers and buyers can hide behind the claim that all software will contain errors, there is less motivation for care in trying to eliminate as many of these errors as possible (Nissenbaum 1994). In many cases there will need to be a balance between the cost of software and the number of errors, and in non-life-threatening systems this does not matter too much (Yourdon 1995). This does not exempt developers and buyers from accountability, but where the line is drawn will determine who is the more accountable. In life-threatening situations clearly minimising errors is more important. Here the balance must be much more toward the number of errors than the cost, but the principles do not change.

SUMMARY

In this chapter we have argued that software developers or owners or both can be held accountable for problems caused by software faults: the developers because they developed it, and the owners to the extent of their knowledge of its possible errors. The discussion considered first the conditions of accountability, then the supposed inevitability of software errors, and finally the question of when "good enough" is good enough.

REFERENCES

ACM Code of Ethics and Professional Conduct. 1992. [On-line]. Available gopher://
ACM.ORG:70/00%5Bthe_files.constitution%5Dbylaw17.txt
ACS Code of Ethics 1993. In electronic format. *IT Practitioner's Handbook.* Darlinghurst, NSW: Australian Computer Society.

Collins, W. Robert, Keith W. Miller, Bethany J. Speilman, and Phillip Wherry. 1994. How good is good enough: An ethical analysis of software construction and use. *Communications of the ACM* 37 (January): 81–91.

Feinberg, Joel. 1970. *Doing and Deserving: Essays in the Theory of Responsibility*. Princeton, NJ: Princeton University Press.

Johnson, Deborah G., and John M. Mulvey. 1995. Accountability and computer decision support systems. *Communications of the ACM* 38 (December): 58–64.

Katz, William A. 1992. *Introduction to Reference Work Volume 2: Reference Services and Reference Processes*. 6th ed. New York: McGraw-Hill.

Kurzweil, Raymond. 1990. *The Age of Intelligent Machines*. Cambridge, MA: MIT Press.

Level 5 Object for Microsoft Windows. Release 2.5, 1992. New York: Information Builders.

Littlewood, Bev, and Lorenzo Strigini. 1992. The risks of software. *Scientific American* 267 (November): 38–43.

Nissenbaum, Helen. 1994. Computing and accountability. *Communications of the ACM* 37 (January): 73–80.

Parnas, David L., A. John van Schouwen, and Shu Po Kwan. 1990. Evaluation of safety-critical software. *Communications of the ACM* 33 (June): 636–48.

Yourdon, Edward. 1995. When good enough software is best. *IEEE Software* 12 (May): 79–81.

FURTHER READING

Dorsett, Robert D. 1994. Risks in Aviation, Part 1. *Communications of the ACM* 37 (January): 154.

Leveson, Nancy G. 1991. Software safety in embedded computer systems. *Communications of the ACM* 34 (February): 34–46.

May, Larry, and Stacy Hoffman, eds. 1991. *Collective Responsibility: Five Decades of Debate in Theoretical and Applied Ethics*. Baltimore, MD: Rowman and Littlefield.

Neumann, Peter G. 1990. Some reflections on a telephone switching problem. *Communications of the ACM* 33 (January): 154.

Samuelson, Pamela. 1993a. Liability for defective electronic information. *Communications of the ACM* 36 (January): 21–26.

---------------------------------- **8** ----------------------------------

What Computers
Should Not Do

> The very asking of the question, "What does a judge (or a psychiatrist) know
> that we cannot tell a computer?" is a monstrous obscenity. That it has to be
> put into print at all, even for the purposes of exposing its morbidity, is a sign
> of the madness of our times. . . . Computers can make judicial decisions,
> computers can make psychiatric judgments. They can flip coins in much more
> sophisticated ways than can the most patient human being. The point is that
> they ought not be given such tasks. (Weizenbaum 1984: 226–27)

The preceding chapter examined accountability for mistakes generated by
computers. In this chapter the emphasis will be on how we as humans perceive ourselves in relation to technology that generates information in a
manner that, on the surface, is not too different from the way we do. High
self-esteem or self-respect is an important ingredient of a good life, something to be discussed in the next chapter. If computers are used in ways that
encourage us to think less of ourselves as humans, then we ought to consider those uses very carefully, even if they have other benefits, such as profitability. In this chapter we will concentrate on the question of using
computers in areas normally involving human judgement. Is this in some
way dehumanising? It might be thought so in two ways. First, it might be
thought dehumanising to take advice from a machine. This in some way
places the machine above us. Second, it might be thought degrading to humans even to suggest or assume that machines *can* make judgements. It
seems to make them equal with us in a slightly humiliating way. We have no
problem with machines being our equals or betters with respect to strength

and speed. But having the ability to make judgements involves intelligence, and this has always been considered a very human attribute. Copernicus moved us away from the centre of the universe. Darwin placed us into the animal kingdom. But at least we still had rationality and intelligence more or less to ourselves, certainly in any quantity. If we now concede that machines share our most unique attribute, what have we left to make us unique? How demoralising and dehumanising, it might be thought!

Two issues concerning dehumanisation will be considered in this chapter. The first is the whole exercise of attempting to develop machines with intelligence. The main problem is a basic assumption of such research, that is, that human intelligence *can* be built into machines. This will be discussed only briefly, in the next section. The second issue concerns the use of machines in situations calling for human judgement. That will be examined in the rest of the chapter.

ARTIFICIAL INTELLIGENCE

This charge of dehumanisation is perhaps most frequently made in the field of Artificial Intelligence (AI). The general claim sometimes made is that the study of AI itself is dehumanising and immoral. It is not easy to know what to make of this, largely because it is so difficult to define the field of AI. One common definition of AI is that it is the science of getting machines, or computer systems, to perform tasks that require intelligence if done by humans (see Minsky 1968: v). But this is obviously too general. Most things that computers do require intelligence if done by humans. Using this definition, even pocket calculators would be intelligent systems. Another common definition of AI is that it is "the study of how to make computers do things which, at the moment, people do better" (Rich and Knight 1991: 3). A problem with this definition is that it seems to imply that if there were no tasks at which people were better, then AI would not exist. But this seems odd. Perhaps a better approach is to describe AI in terms of more specific topics that form the core of AI research, for example, machine learning, reasoning, natural language understanding, and perception. This still does not clearly distinguish AI from the rest of computing, but it does highlight the main areas of research and development. The dehumanisation charge then might be that research into and development of systems that centre around these areas is in some way demeaning. The claim is often stated in terms of self-respect. Attempting to incorporate human-like intelligence into machines, or even claiming that it can be done, suggests that humans are no more than mere machines, endangering human self-respect. This claim, as vague as it is, is naturally resisted by many in the AI profession, who argue that the attempt to build intelligent machines actually enhances our view of humanity because we come to realise just how complex we are.

Margaret Boden, defending AI against this kind of attack, argues that "the prime metaphysical significance of artificial intelligence is that it can *counteract* the subtly dehumanising influence of natural science" (Boden 1987: 473). Her argument is essentially this: Artificial intelligence assumes that it is possible to build intelligence into a machine, so machines can become "human-like" in that sense. The programming required to produce (or simulate) even very moderate intelligence is complex, and the amount of knowledge required is considerable. Accordingly, if a person is likened to this kind of machine, nothing is implied that suggests that humans are merely mechanistic and purely deterministic automata. Artificial Intelligence as a discipline recognises that a mind of some sort controls, or at least influences, what the body does, so the view of humans embodied here is not a behaviouristic one. Further, we are not merely products of our environment. There is room for choice, responsibility for actions, and other things that we might consider essential to humanness. This is not to suggest that intelligent machines have all of these human characteristics, but suggesting that we are like such machines is very different from saying that we are very simple machines.

In the final chapter the question of whether or not machines *can* be intelligent will be examined in much more detail. For the argument of this chapter, it is enough that they are used for certain kinds of task. The use of computers in psychotherapy will be considered first, and then the employment of expert systems for library reference work.

ELIZA AND PSYCHOTHERAPY

ELIZA is a much-discussed program designed to simulate a psychotherapist. Following is a short extract from a consultation with ELIZA, whose responses are in upper case.

Men are all alike.

IN WHAT WAY?

They're always bugging us about something or other.

CAN YOU THINK OF A SPECIFIC EXAMPLE?

Well my boyfriend made me come here.

YOUR BOYFRIEND MADE YOU COME HERE.

He says I'm depressed much of the time.

I'M SORRY TO HEAR THAT YOU ARE DEPRESSED.

It's true, I am unhappy.

DO YOU THINK THAT COMING HERE WILL HELP YOU NOT TO BE UNHAPPY?

I need some help, that much seems certain.

WHAT WOULD IT MEAN TO YOU IF YOU GOT SOME
  HELP?

Perhaps I could learn to get along with my mother.

TELL ME MORE ABOUT YOUR FAMILY.

My mother takes care of me.

WHO ELSE TAKES CARE OF YOU?

My father.

YOUR FATHER.

You are like my father in some ways.

WHAT RESEMBLANCE DO YOU SEE?

You are not very aggressive but I think that you don't want me
  to notice you.

WHAT MAKES YOU THINK THAT I AM NOT VERY AG-
  GRESSIVE?

You don't argue with me.

WHY DO YOU THINK THAT I DON'T ARGUE WITH YOU?

You are afraid of me.

DOES IT PLEASE YOU TO THINK THAT I AM AFRAID OF
  YOU?

My father is afraid of everybody.

WHAT ELSE COMES TO YOUR MIND WHEN YOU THINK
  OF YOUR FATHER?

Bullies.

DOES THAT HAVE ANYTHING TO DO WITH THE FACT
  THAT YOUR BOYFRIEND MADE YOU COME HERE?
  (Weizenbaum 1984: 3–4)

While this appears quite impressive at first, sensible responses are obtained only within strict limits. However, within these limits there is some
appearance of intelligence.

   In order now to focus the dehumanisation objection (at least as it arises
in connection with AI), we will concentrate on one argument raised by
Joseph Weizenbaum:

   All projects that propose to substitute a computer system for a
   human function that involves interpersonal respect, understanding, and love ... are obscene. ... Their ... very contem-
   plation ought to give rise to feelings of disgust in every
   civilised person. (1976: 268–69)

He argues, or at least states, that using computer programs such as ELIZA for psychotherapy is bad, that is, immoral. However, that this use is immoral is not obvious. We use machines to assist humans in all sorts of tasks, so why not in psychotherapy as well? If people require this sort of help, and if they can get it more readily if machines are employed, and if the results are satisfactory, surely it is a good thing, or so it appears. Why, then, might it be a bad thing? There seem to be three possibilities:

1. it does not work;
2. it makes the condition worse;
3. regardless of whether it works or not, it is dehumanising to get this sort of help from a machine.

The first and second possibilities are important; if either of them is true, such machines should not be used. Empirical studies are needed to verify them. The third possibility is more interesting from a moral point of view. The question now is, why is it dehumanising? It cannot be merely the fact that it involves communication with a machine. We do that frequently, with no qualms. (Perhaps we should have some, but that is another issue.) We talk to and listen to telephone answering machines, to tape recorders, and to computers when we use electronic mail. But, the reply will be, in these cases our message is intended for a human, and if a reply is required, that reply will ultimately come from a human. The machine is merely a tool to facilitate human communication.

It is true that strictly speaking we are not in such cases communicating *with* a machine, but rather *by means of* a machine. But the situation seems not quite so clear. If I speak to a Chinese speaker through a translator, am I communicating with the translator or just by means of the translator? Perhaps I am communicating with the translator because she must make some conscious effort to understand me in order to translate. But what if the translator is a machine? If I am communicating with the human translator, why not also with the machine version? But if I am communicating with the machine translator, it is not easy to see why I am not also communicating with the telephone or the tape recorder when I use those devices. Certainly the machine translator does something in a way that the telephone and tape recorder do not, but why does that matter? Perhaps because it contains some of the knowledge of a human. It is not obvious, however, that this should make a difference. In all cases a message from one human passes to another via some electrical impulses.

In the case of a telephone or tape recorder we are not baring our soul to, or trusting the advice of, a machine. It is true that in the case of ELIZA-type programs, there is no human who will ultimately hear and respond to the patient. But it could be argued that any advice really comes from one or more humans who developed the program, or from the humans whose knowledge is in the program. The problem then might be that the patient is not talking to the psychotherapist. However, we often get help and advice from books or magazines. Here the help and advice has a human source, but we do not talk to the advice giver. The advice is packaged and we must access it. This seems not too different from the computer case. It still has a human source. Suppose that it is argued that the computer "creates" advice in a way that a book does not. In a sense then, the advice is really coming from a machine. This raises interesting questions about machine creativity, but suppose that a machine can be really creative. (This is not a completely implausible supposition, but of course an account of creativity is needed.) Wherein lies the problem now? It seems to lie in the fact that we are talking to, and getting advice from, a nonhuman. But plenty of people talk to, and get help and comfort from nonhumans, frequently in the form of animals. The therapeutic value of pets is often appreciated.

One possible response to the above example is that in the case of animals, we might get comfort and a form of friendship, but not advice on how to solve our problems. This is true, but it is not obvious why this distinction between different sorts of help should be drawn. Perhaps we should get advice only from creatures who are enough like us to understand us. This may be a prerequisite for giving useful advice. But it is not obvious why this should be so. Another response might be that animals are alive while machines are not. We can assume that machines are not and never will be alive, but it is still unclear why this is important. It assumes that while it is unobjectionable to get help (i.e., psychotherapeutic help) from nonhumans that are alive, it is objectionable to get such help from nonhumans that are nonliving. Both of the responses in this paragraph have the ring of arbitrariness.

Weizenbaum might argue however, that all of this misses his point, which he presents in two rhetorical questions: (1) "Do we wish to encourage people to lead their lives on the basis of patent fraud, charlatanism, and unreality?" and (2) "Do we really believe that it helps people living in our already overly machine-like world to prefer the therapy administered by machines to that given by people?" (1976: 269) The first question raises several others. First, if someone's life is improved, why does it matter if this improvement came about as a result of "patent fraud, charlatanism, and unreality"? A second is what the fraud, charlatanism, and unreality are in this context. Presumably Weizenbaum believes they consist in the fact that computer systems cannot encompass interpersonal respect, understanding, and love. Is this so?

It is presumably true that computer systems at least as we currently know them are unable to show respect or have feelings of love. And any understanding they have is rudimentary at best and not really an understanding of the human situation. Perhaps they never will have the latter. But how different is this from the actual situation with human psychotherapists? Certainly they are, as human beings, capable of all of these feelings and emotions. But there is not normally love between a patient and the professional psychotherapist. It is also unclear how much mutual respect there can be in a situation in which someone is paying for this sort of advice or emotional help. The situation is very different from that in which I "bare my breast" to a friend. And how much understanding is really possible? The psychotherapist after all hardly knows the patient in most cases. The situation of the professional psychotherapist is not very different from that of a prostitute. Both are providing a service which must be bought because basic human needs could not be satisfied in more loving, caring, and probably satisfying ways.

The argument here is not that professional psychotherapy is immoral. Rather the suggestion is that we can and do get help in situations in which interpersonal respect, understanding, and love are lacking. I can get help from a book even though the author does not know me, let alone love me and understand me. And this author may have total contempt for the readers, intending by the book solely to make money. Thus it is not clear just what the fraud consists of, or if there is fraud, why psychotherapy is not also fraudulent. Perhaps, however, such systems are fraudulent in that while they cannot really help, they give the impression that they can, or at least their supporters make claims that they can. If this is so, then peddlers of ELIZA-like systems are no better than peddlers of snake oil. This criticism holds only if computer systems can never give good psychological advice. The problem here for Weizenbaum is that he does not deny that this may be possible. But where is the fraud then? The systems, or their supporters, are only claiming what is legitimate, that is, these systems can help. This leads us back to the question of whether, if the systems help people, it matters if in some other sense they may be fraudulent.

The suggestion is, though not stated explicitly by Weizenbaum, that even if people are happier or in some sense better off because of computerised psychotherapy, they acquire that state in an illegitimate or dehumanising manner. The situation is akin to that in which some desirable state is induced by drugs. The real issue now is whether or not it matters how desirable states are acquired. This will be the subject of the next section.

Weizenbaum's question (2) is "Do we really believe that it helps people to . . . prefer therapy administered by machines to that given by people?" One answer is obvious. Of course, if the machine administered therapy is as good as and cheaper or more readily available than that given by people, or if it is actually better, it does help to prefer the machine delivered version. Perhaps, however, his point is deeper. It might be that there is something wrong with society if people prefer interacting with machines rather than with other people. In this situation something valuable is lost, namely human interaction. Here he is on firmer ground, but the argument no longer is limited to Artificial Intelligence applications. Automatic teller machines reduce human contact, and the "Information Super Highway" with its possibilities for buying, banking, and getting all sorts of information without leaving home, will mean that direct human-to-human contact will be even less prevalent. This is not an attempt to show that Weizenbaum's argument leads to an absurdity. It is, rather, an attempt to show that the one interpretation that makes his second objection plausible has wider application than he seems to intend.

This discussion of Weizenbaum's objections to the use of computers in psychotherapy has led to two substantive issues. One is the question of whether or not it matters how we induce desirable states of mind. The other is the issue of computers reducing the need for much human interaction. This is really where the moral discussions begin.

Inducing Desirable States of Mind

Does it matter how desirable mental states are induced? In general we seem to think that it does, but perhaps this is just because the most common case of such inducement is drug use, with all of its accompanying problems. But suppose that desirable states could be acquired artificially without any harmful side effects. For example, suppose that I could have the experience of travelling through the Andes with the aid of virtual reality. Would this experience in some way be poorer than the real thing and why? Consider these four propositions:

1. pleasurable states should be the result of some effort;
2. they are more satisfying if they are the result of some effort;
3. there is the lack of danger, which might reduce the amount of excitement;
4. there might always be the doubt that it was exactly like the real thing.

It is not clear why (1) is true. It might be true that effort increases the pleasure, but to say that is not to maintain that pleasure *should* always be associated with effort. And (4) could in principle always be verified by real travel through the Andes. So we can ignore both of those. There is more worry with (2) and (3), though. It is probably true that in general, the more effort that we put into something the more rewarding we find it, as we will see in chapter 9. If we constantly get our pleasure through artificially induced states, we lose the sense of achievement that we get when we work for something. This is not an argument against inducing pleasure by means of virtual reality (something to be discussed more

fully in chapter 10), but it is an argument against attaining all our pleasure that way if we have alternatives. A similar argument applies in the
case of danger. I am likely to get more satisfaction from overcoming my
fear of some danger and using my skill to overcome the danger itself than
I am if there is no challenge. But this is only an argument against never
exposing oneself to the real thing and always limiting oneself to virtual
reality. In both of these examples, perhaps the belief that one is making
some effort, or that one is in some danger, could be induced. However,
deception would be inherent in this, and this deception would normally
be objectionable.

Some might agree that getting pleasurable states by means of machines
is not too bad, even if a little sad, but maintain that this is different from
inducing mental states to do with, say, peace of mind and contentment.
These states seem deeper than pleasure, and we hope them to be more
long-lasting; would it be possible to induce them safely and effectively by
artificial means? Drugs may induce them, but often with unwelcome side-
effects; would a machine be any better? But if there were a completely
safe, artificial way of becoming contented, would using that method be
objectionable? It is not clear why it would be, any more so than in the case
of pleasure. It does however seem to be a less satisfactory way of becoming contented. My contentment comes from things like achievement, love,
friendship, and so on. Inducing the belief in all of this would seem to involve unavoidably some sort of deception or unreality. Constantly living
like this would almost certainly affect my interaction with the real world
and probably make the induced contentment even more necessary. So
there do seem to be more serious problems with inducing these states
than in the case of pleasure. However, it does not follow that it is always
wrong to induce them artificially. Just as with pleasure, sometimes it
might be the least bad alternative.

How does this relate to Weizenbaum's argument? His argument, we
saw, was that it is wrong to use machines in situations involving human
judgement, love, and the like. One substantial issue in his argument is that
it matters how psychological or mental states are produced. We have seen
that it does matter, sometimes anyway, but it is not clear that it does in the
ELIZA-type situation he discusses. There are no side effects as there commonly are in the use of drugs, and no deception, or there need be none.
Even if the treatment is not as good as the "real thing" administered by a
human, it may still be valuable and better than nothing.

Computers and Human Interaction

The second substantial point to emerge from the discussion of Weizenbaum's argument was that using machines in the manner to which he objects lessens direct human interaction, and this does seem beyond dispute.

As mentioned earlier, automatic teller machines remove the need to talk with a human teller. Increasingly we will be able to bank, shop, and get entertainment without leaving home, through the Internet. This is all convenient, but it comes at a cost, and the cost is direct human interaction. Does this matter? It almost certainly does. We humans have evolved as basically social creatures. We generally prefer to live in groups. Much of our social interaction comes about as a result of our normal actions in our daily lives. However, the less need there is to go to the banks, the shops, the cinemas, and so on, the more isolated we become. At the same time, of course, the potential for indirect interaction has been increased markedly. Via the Internet we are able to talk with friends and colleagues all over the world in a way never before possible. But however useful and interesting this is, this kind of interaction is not a real substitute for "flesh and blood" interaction. There is, then, some point to Weizenbaum's worry here. However, again it does not show that the systems he describes are bad. (Some of the points in this section will be developed further in the next chapter.)

What Computers Should Not Do

Weizenbaum does not establish that there is anything that computers should not do. It might be better if we did not need them for tasks involving love and understanding, but it does not follow that their use here is wrong. What does emerge from the two substantive issues hidden in his argument is that somehow we need to develop new social structures or ways of living and doing things that compensate for the losses created by various kinds of computer use. Computers should not be introduced willy-nilly without serious study of the social consequences.

EXPERT SYSTEMS AND HUMAN DECISION-MAKING

As we have seen, Weizenbaum believes that it is immoral to substitute a computer system for a human function that involves interpersonal respect, understanding, and love. Some proposed (and actual) expert system applications come close to being in this category. The one we will consider is that of an expert system replacing a librarian at the library's reference desk. Reference librarians must on occasion make judgements involving the understanding of humans, or so we will argue. They must judge, we suggest, whether or not they should assist someone in finding some particular material. The question of relevance here then is whether it is right to replace such a person with a computer system. Or is this in some way degrading to humans? (see Weckert and Ferguson 1993)

The central issue is whether reference librarians *should* attempt to satisfy all patron inquiries. The traditional view is that they should. Foskett puts it this way:

During the reference service, the librarian ought virtually to vanish as an individual person, except in so far as his personality sheds light on the working of the library. He must be the reader's alter ego, immersed in his politics, his religion, his morals. He must have the ability to participate in the reader's enthusiasms and to devote himself wholly and wholeheartedly to whatever cause the reader has at the time of the enquiry. He must put himself in the reader's shoes. (Foskett 1962: 10)

In a similar vein the ALA's *Code of Ethics* says that librarians must provide "... accurate, unbiased, and courteous responses to *all* requests" (our emphasis) (I). It is easier to find statements like these than it is to find supporting arguments, but the following four are used. Here they will only be mentioned. (1) First, there is the equity argument. Librarians should supply information without bias, that is, should provide an equal service to all their patrons and avoid differential treatment. (2) Second, the librarian has no right to exercise censorship, which in this context is a form of paternalism. Even if some authority has the right to withhold information from library users, the reference librarian certainly does not. (3) A third argument is that a library user has a right to any information that is in the library. (4) Finally, there is the pragmatic argument. This states that by withholding information, the librarian is not really helping the situation anyway; library users who really want some information will find some way of acquiring it.

This hard-line position is not taken by the Australian Library and Information Association (ALIA). ALIA's qualified view is expressed in its *Statement on Professional Ethics*, which says that librarians and library technicians "must provide the highest level of service through appropriate and usefully organised collections, equitable service policies and skilful, accurate and unbiased responses to all *legitimate* requests for assistance" (our emphasis) (1992: 77). Here, of course, everything depends on how "legitimate" is understood.

The view that reference librarians should not always answer patrons' requests is argued by Robert Hauptman, who writes: "the actions of a subgroup [reference librarians] cannot contravene the tenets by which the main group lives (Wiener 1987: 161). In other words, moral obligations to one's fellow human beings override professional obligations. (This issue of conflict between professional and wider social obligations was raised in chapter 2.) A librarian in certain circumstances has a moral obligation not to, for example, give help in finding material on bomb or drug manufacture, or suicide. If there is overwhelming evidence that the information requested will be used to harm the patron or another person, it should not be given. According to Hauptman again: "To abjure an ethical commitment in favor of anything, is to abjure one's individual responsibility" (1976: 627).

We would suggest that when the librarian is asked for information, she should use her judgement (moral or otherwise) and on some occasions (albeit in exceptional circumstances) may refuse help to a patron. One argument for this is that humans are gregarious. We like to live in societies. We enjoy the company of others of our species. To live happily and well in societies we need to adopt certain codes of behaviour. We need to be able to trust most of the people most of the time. One cannot live comfortably while continually fearing attack from everyone else. Care is also important. A society cannot function to the benefit of most of its members if no one cares for anyone else. One expression of this care must be the protection of the innocent, both by the state and by individuals. If we have good reason to believe that a certain action will harm other humans, we have an obligation not to perform it and to inhibit others from performing it. After all, we would like our fellow humans to do the same for us if we were the ones to be harmed.

John Swan also says that there may be cases in which he would refuse help to a user: "If the would-be bomber came to the reference desk uttering threats, if the would-be suicide seeking a how-to manual showed visible signs of depression, if a student openly admitted wanting help in plagiary, the librarian would be thrust into the position of weighing principles" (Wiener 1987: 162). Is it ethical to help a student find a how-to-commit-suicide manual? In answering this question Paul Wiener argues that it all depends on how the user looks and behaves. He suggests that "since we're only human, let that be the basis of helping each other, not cut-and-dried 'professional' guidelines that treat information as if all of it belonged in a computer" (Wiener 1983: 643). This brings us conveniently back to expert systems.

For those who hold to the extreme version of the traditional position that a reference librarian should answer every request for information, regardless of the perceived harm that might be caused to others, there is no problem here. The expert system may indeed be an improvement on the prying human intermediary. In that case, the following discussion of expert systems will be misguided. But we have argued that this extreme position is untenable and continue on the basis that there may well be cases in which the human librarian will justifiably refuse a request for assistance. If we accept that a person's civic or moral obligations can override the professional obligation to supply information on request, then the introduction of expert systems to act as reference advisers does raise problems.

An expert system is a computer program designed to simulate the function of an expert in some very specialised area. Typically it will contain the expert knowledge in the form of rules. An example of a rule in a system being built to give advice to vineyard managers is:

IF petiole test value is less than 0.12

AND the variety is Pinot Noir

AND the Past Test Result is less than or equal to 0.20 or is not
   available

THEN the sample indicates phosphorus is deficient. (Scott and
   Weckert 1996: 575)

These systems will ask questions, and on the basis of the answers, together with the rules and perhaps other data, give advice in much the way
that a human expert would.

An expert system for reference is a piece of computer software that is
designed to duplicate the expertise of a reference librarian. This is the
most common area of expert system research and development in libraries. In principle, such a system should be able to do all that the human
can do in the field of reference. Such a system can determine the wants of
the user and advise her where to find the material that she seeks, or perhaps supply the information. In this sense the system simulates, or behaves like, a reference librarian.

Expert systems for reference can simulate the behaviour of a reference
librarian, but only up to a point, in their present stage of sophistication.
They can do a good job of asking questions which have definite answers
and of locating information. They are not so good at vague questions and
very poor with nonverbal communication, which, J. J. Mills suggests, is so
important (1992: 10–11). Nor can they make judgements about whether
some request for information ought to be satisfied. A good expert system
might satisfy the ALA code of ethics, and it might make Foskett extremely
happy, but it could not behave in a way that would satisfy Hauptman, or
us. Such a system would give any information it had to anyone who
asked. It would truly be "the reader's alter ego, immersed in his politics,
his religion, his morals." But as we have already seen, there is good reason
to believe that the reference librarian should not be so morally detached.

How can the problem be overcome? The obvious reply is that expert
systems should not be used for reference until they can make moral judgements, which is quite likely never to eventuate. The best that could be
done with current technology is that either such systems are developed
only in uncontroversial areas, or when information on certain topics was
requested, they would either give no information, or better, they would
tell the user to ask a librarian. But it would be hard to know where to draw
the line. Many legitimate but mundane requests would be channelled to
the librarian or not answered by the system at all, taking away much of
the purpose of having it.

Questions of a psychological type could be asked in response to reference inquiries of certain kinds in order to ascertain whether or not the library patron has any unpleasant motives. Users would probably baulk at
this, even if it could be done subtly, and it would also make the reference
procedure much slower. In any case, how would the system know when to

ask these questions? Many requests on these topics will be quite legitimate, and it would be unnecessary and intrusive to so interrogate all inquirers.

Future developments in AI may come to the rescue. Consider again the conditions under which the reference librarian might refuse to help a library user. One condition is the topic, which might be potentially dangerous to the user or to someone else, and another is the behaviour of the user. This behaviour might manifest itself in bodily movements, facial expressions, voice, language, and so on. According to J. J. Mills, 65 percent of social meaning is communicated nonverbally. Study of the nonverbal component includes (1) paralinguistics, which studies nonlexical vocal components of speech such as tone of voice, (2) kinesics, or the study of so-called body language, and (3) proxemics, which is the study of time and space, and in the reference situation looks at aspects such as the territoriality of the information desk. Any expert system in reference work must cope not only with the complexities of the reference collection or sources, but also with the complexities of the system/user interaction. Cues received from these other sources might indicate to a human being such characteristics as extreme nervousness, aggression, tension, and so on. Present expert systems cannot cope with these. Advanced vision systems are necessary in order to get information from the appearance of a person. Speech recognition and natural language understanding systems require much more sophistication than they currently have if they are to get relevant information from voice and language. Productive research and development is occurring in all of these fields, but there is little prospect that they will be incorporated into small-scale expert systems at the required level in the near future.

We have argued that reference librarians do sometimes have a responsibility to withhold information from library patrons. While this might be a rare occurrence, it does have implications for the introduction of expert or other fully computerised reference systems. The ethically unconsidered introduction of these systems presupposes an answer to the question of whether or not reference librarians should ever refuse to give information, and it is the wrong answer. It seems to us that one positive thing that the introduction of expert systems for reference does is force us to think carefully about the moral responsibility of reference librarians. The advent of expert systems for reference has made consideration of the issue more urgent. Our proposal is not that expert systems for reference have no place, but rather that there is a need for examination of more than just efficiency or profitability, something noted throughout this book in a number of contexts.

SUMMARY

In this chapter the concern was with some uses of computers that might be considered questionable. We responded to the objection that if machines are thought to be intelligent enough to be able to make judgements and give advice usually received only from human sources, then this is dehumanising and damaging to our self-esteem as humans. In considering Weizenbaum's arguments we found little to suggest that computers should not be used in the way that he attacks, although it might be better if there were no need for that use. But choosing second best when there is no alternative is not necessarily dehumanising. It may do little for our self-esteem, of course, if we know that we *must* choose second best. In the second case, that of the library expert system, there is a reason to be very careful before introducing or using such a system. The reason is not that such systems are dehumanising as they stand, but that they are not capable of making relevant judgements about a library user's intentions or state of mind. Computer systems can be used in ways that are likely to be dehumanising and result in loss of self-esteem, but this does not follow necessarily from the use of intelligent systems, or from their use in situations in which they make human-like judgements.

REFERENCES

ALA Code of Ethics. 1995. [On-line]. Available gopher://gopher.ala.org:70/00/alagophii/ethics.txt

Australian Library and Information Association. 1992. *1991/1992 Handbook.* Canberra: Australian Library and Information Association.

Boden, Margaret. 1987. *Artificial Intelligence and Natural Man.* 2d ed. New York: Basic Books.

Foskett, D. J. 1962. *The Creed of a Librarian: No Politics, No Religion, No Morals.* London: Library Association.

Hauptman, Robert. 1976. Professionalism or culpability? An experiment in ethics. *Wilson Library Bulletin* 50: 626–27.

Mills, J. J. 1992. *Information Resources and Services in Australia.* 2d ed. Wagga Wagga: Centre for Information Studies.

Minsky, M. L., ed. 1968. *Semantic Information Processing.* Cambridge, Mass: MIT Press.

Rich, Elaine, and Kevin Knight. 1991. *Artificial Intelligence.* 2d ed. New York: McGraw-Hill.

Scott, Jan, and John Weckert. 1996. Expert system explanation: A methodology for generation. In *Critical Technology: Proceedings of the Third World Congress on Expert Systems,* ed. Jae Kyu Lee, Jay Liebowitz, and Young Moon Chae. New York: Cognizant Communication Corporation, pp. 569–76.

Weckert, John, and Stuart Ferguson. 1993. Ethics, reference librarians and expert systems. *Australian Library Journal* 42 (August): 172–81.

Weizenbaum, Joseph. 1976. ELIZA—A computer program for the study of natural language communication between man and machine. *Communications of the ACM* 9 (January): 36–45.

Weizenbaum, Joseph. 1984. *Computer Power and Human Reason: From Judgement to Calculation.* Harmondsworth: Penguin Books.

Wiener, Paul B. 1983. Is it ethical to help a student find a how-to-commit-suicide manual, and is that all you do? *American Libraries* 14: 643.

Wiener, Paul B. 1987. Mad bombers and ethical librarians: A dialogue with Robert Hauptman and John Swan. *Catholic Library World* 58: 161–63.

FURTHER READING

Boden, Margaret. 1990. *The Creative Mind: Myths and Mechanisms*. London: Weidenfield and Nicolson.

Collins, H. M. 1990. *Artificial Experts: Social Knowledge and Intelligent Machines*. Cambridge, MA: MIT Press.

Crevier, Daniel. 1993. *AI: The Tumultuous History of the Search for Artificial Intelligence*. New York: Basic Books.

Forester, Tom, and Perry Morrison. 1995. 2d ed. *Computer Ethics: Cautionary Tales and Ethical Dilemmas in Computing*. Cambridge, MA: MIT Press, chapter 7.

9

Quality of Life and Work

At the 1940 World's Fair, American industry promised that computers and automation would eliminate toil, freeing citizens to pursue higher goals. In the 1980s the promise was reduced burden on office workers, and new career opportunities. In the 1990s, the computer industry is vaunting an information revolution that will allow incredible communication between people. (Leinfuss 1995: 16)

We are frequently given the impression, particularly in the popular press, that computers enhance or even enrich life. In other words, they improve the environment in which we live and work. The draft guidelines of the ACM code of ethics also promote this view, stating that "computing's major value is its potential to enhance the well-being of individuals and society as a whole" (1992: 95). This statement is not included in the current code, but it does still state that "As an ACM member I will contribute to society and human well-being" (1.1). The ACS code contains a similar proposition: "I will strive to enhance the quality of life of those affected by my work" (4). There is, however, a group of problems that revolve around the question of whether the introduction of computers might actually make life less satisfying for the people affected, or even be dehumanising. If some new technology does not improve the general quality of life, it is not at all clear that it ought to be introduced. When it comes to computer technology, people argue both ways. Some think that our lives have improved, while others doubt it. In this chapter we want to consider first the quality of life. Is there anything that can be said about what constitutes the good life that is relevant to the discussion of computer technology? We will then turn to some ways that computers can affect work, because work plays such an important part in the life of an inhabitant of the modern industrialised world. Our interest is not centred on how the introduction of computers has affected the working lives of information professionals—it goes without saying that their work has changed dramatically. Librarians, for example, now must be able to cope with CD-ROM and on-line databases and computer-based catalogues as well as (or in some cases instead of) book and card catalogues. Computing professionals of course would not even exist without the technology. The concern in this chapter is with work in general.

THE GOOD LIFE

Whether our life is of satisfactory quality depends both on what our life is like—our material circumstances, health, and so on—and on what we want out of life. It is worth noting here that "quality of life" must not be confused with "standard of living," as that phrase is commonly used. Economists and others measure, or attempt to measure, standards of living by looking at income, housing, education, health care, and the like. While these things clearly are related to a person's quality of life, they are only part of the story. At best they are a prerequisite for a good quality of life. Quality of life cannot be measured in the way that standard of living can be, any more than our enjoyment of a piece of music or a sunset can be measured. One can enjoy a high standard of living but still lead a life of poor quality.

What constitutes a "quality life" or a "good life" cannot be defined precisely, but we need to make things a little clearer if we want to say anything useful about how computers fit into the greater scheme of things. We can say that our quality of life improves the closer that we approach the good life. Well, what is the good life? Obviously different people have different ideas as to what makes up the good life. As the song says, "Happiness is different things to different people," and so is the good life. But there is a bit more that can be said. First, we can try to see if there is anything that is universally, or almost universally, thought to be part of the good life, and then see if there are ways to evaluate different tastes.

Is there anything that would almost universally be included as part of the good life? Given the diversity of people's tastes, this question may seem odd or quaint. But there are a few things that can quite plausibly be included. We all need adequate food, not only to survive, but to have the health and energy to do the things that we enjoy. The same can be said of shelter. Most humans are gregarious. We enjoy the company of others of our species. That is just the way that we have evolved. Therefore, the good life for most of us involves living in a situation that is conducive to having a rewarding social life. We also enjoy achieving, whether that involves building houses, painting pictures, devising personal financial strategies, teaching children, or a host of other things. We need to do things that we find satisfying and that give us some pride in ourselves and our achievements. Any good life must allow this. Finally, we must be able to experience the beauty in our environment, whether that be the natural environment or the social one or both.

What has been said so far about the good life says nothing about what is good to achieve, what sort of friends are best, or what we should consider beautiful. But these things do have some bearing on the discussion of computers and quality of life. Computers change things, so it is important to know whether these changes have a bearing on quality of life as opposed to merely on standard of living. The question here then is: Are some things inherently better than others? For example, is Bach better than the Rolling Stones, or Rembrandt better than Jackson Pollock? The normal reaction to this issue these days is to say that of course there is no way that one is better than the other and that to maintain anything to the contrary is just elitist rubbish. But it is worth a closer look before coming to this conclusion.

According to J. S. Mill, some pleasures are worth more than others. "The pleasures of the intellect," he says, "of the feelings and imagination, and of the moral sentiments, [have] a much higher value as pleasures" than "those of mere sensation" (1863: 11). By this he means not simply that the "higher" pleasures tend to be longer-lasting, more likely to lead to further pleasures, and so on—true though he thinks this is—but that they are higher in quality and more worthwhile regardless of the amount of pleasure to be expected. Quality is different from quantity and much more important. And so, says Mill, "It is better to be a human being dissatisfied than a pig satisfied; better to be Socrates dissatisfied than a fool satisfied" (1863: 14).

In this Mill differed from Jeremy Bentham, another great utilitarian philosopher, who remarked that "quantity of pleasure being equal, pushpin is as good as poetry" (pushpin is a simple table game). Bentham would say then that if it is a choice between being Socrates *dissatisfied* and being the fool or pig *satisfied*, then, other things being equal, one should choose the latter. But in fact, as Mill and Bentham would agree, things are seldom equal. Certain activities may require more effort than others, and the development of various faculties of perception and judgement may require very great effort, but yield great rewards. The pleasures of the intellect—academic study or mastery of difficult problems in computer engineering or programming—may be very great indeed. Or consider the enjoyment gained from good wine as opposed to cheap wine. To the uninitiated they may be equally enjoyable. However, to the wine connoisseur the good wine will give much greater satisfaction. There will be a complexity and depth of tastes, smells, and colours entirely lacking from the other. Here too effort is rewarded with increased pleasure; the enjoyment of good wine depends on taking the time to learn to notice the complexities. In many cases the effort required is mental, which might suggest that the pleasures giving the greatest rewards for effort will be intellectual. But (despite Mill, who ranked "mental" pleasures well above "bodily" ones both quantitatively and qualitatively) this need not be so. The pleasure of diving, for example, is a very bodily one, and a complicated dive is presumably much more satisfying to perform successfully than a simple one and certainly more enjoyable to watch.

Thus we may argue on utilitarian grounds for the value of effort, in developing skills of varying kinds, without having to go along with Mill's qualitative distinction between higher and lower pleasures. We may, that is, hold that such effort tends to increase pleasure anyway, and Mill would agree with this too. However, what if it really is a choice between being Socrates dissatisfied and being a fool satisfied? (Imagine a brain operation, or a drug, that will put you permanently into one state or the other). Mill thought that one should choose the former, and that virtually everyone "competently acquainted" with both kinds of life would actually do so, which proved to Mill that it is the better choice and that its pleasures are better than the fool's. Two thousand years earlier Aristotle asked himself a similar question and answered it similarly: Nobody, he said, "would choose to pass through life with the mental outlook of a child, even if he continued to take unlimited pleasure in the things that children like" (1971: 292–93). And so, says Aristotle, pleasure cannot be the only thing good for its own sake. Other things such as sight, memory, and knowledge are good for their own sakes too, and if we had to choose between having our present intellect and having much more pleasure but much less intellect then we would and should choose the former. Mill thought that we ought to distinguish higher and lower pleasures, but did not see that such a distinction (and the view that Socrates' life, even if dissatisfied, is superior to the fool's satisfied one) really points to Aristotle's conclusion: That pleasure is *not* the only good.

Be this as it may, one might argue for the value of effort in developing our intellectual and discriminatory skills either (i) on the Benthamite utilitarian ground that this is likely to give us (and perhaps others indirectly) more pleasure, or (ii) on the Millian utilitarian ground that it will yield pleasure of a higher quality, or (iii) on the Aristotelian ground that the development and exercise of these skills is valuable in itself, an important aspect of the good life for a rational human being quite apart from the pleasure it may yield. The Millian ground is perhaps difficult to keep distinct from the other two. But when we think of the quality of life and of things that may improve or reduce it, we may perhaps have any one or two or all three of these criteria in mind.

COMPUTERS AND WORK

As was mentioned earlier, in Western industrial societies people tend to identify with, and be identified by, their jobs. We are first and foremost secretaries, librarians, philosophers, plasterers, computer scientists, farmers. Our jobs largely determine our status in society, our self-esteem, our lifestyle, and our income. The impact of computers on work is an essential consideration, therefore, when looking at computers and quality of life. Computers affect work in a variety of ways: the number of jobs, the type of job and the level of skill required, and telecommuting, to name just the three to be considered here. Surveillance of workers is also an issue, but that was discussed in an earlier chapter. The question of whether or not computers empower workers is one which we will not discuss (see Clement 1994; Panteli and Corbett 1995).

Number of Jobs

Whether computers create more jobs than they eliminate is a moot point. What is not questionable is that their introduction eliminates some jobs and creates others (see Forester and Morrison 1995 for more discussion). If on balance the number of jobs decreases, the question of computer introduction needs to be considered very carefully. Unemployment in a Western industrial society verges on being a tragedy, not so much because of loss or absence of a wage or salary, which is bad enough, but more because of loss of self-identity, self-esteem, personal confidence, and the like. If on balance the overall number of jobs remains about the same, there is still cause for some concern. This is because the jobs that are created may not be able to be filled by those whose jobs have gone. A clerk, typist, or assembly line worker will not be able to become a computer programmer, network manager, or systems designer without considerable training. And if there is not financial assistance for the training, such people may not be able to move into those and related fields at all.

Whose responsibility is it to do something about these issues of unemployment and training? Clearly there will be no halt to the spread of computer technology. Employers are not likely to delay or abandon introduction of a new technology if they see improved profits from the introduction. This of course does not absolve them of responsibility, but it is not theirs alone. Given that we all, except those who lose their jobs, stand to benefit from more efficiency in better goods and services at lower prices (at least in principle), we should all bear some of the burden for retraining or other measures to give meaningful work to the unemployed. Even if there is a net gain in jobs as a result of computer technology, this issue will arise, though of course less acutely. It seems blatantly immoral to sacrifice a proportion of the population, even if a small one, just so that the rest can live a little better, where "to live a little better" means to have a higher standard of living and not necessarily a better quality of life. On the other side of the ledger, those who lose their jobs definitely suffer a loss in quality of life, unless they are retrained and can find new jobs at least as fulfilling as the ones they lost.

Types of Job and Levels of Skill

The introduction of computer technology also affects those who keep their employment. In some cases boring and dangerous jobs are eliminated. Computers are very good at doing repetitive tasks that humans find boring, certainly after performing them for a time. They are useful in situations in which there is danger to people, because they do not make mistakes (if they are programmed properly) as a result of fatigue or loss of concentration. And any danger to computers themselves is presumably less serious than danger to human workers because of the greater importance of human well-being (but see chapter 11). However, they can also have the effect of replacing jobs requiring some skill with ones requiring very little. Take shop assistants for example. Once their jobs required skill in arithmetic to work out the change to give customers. Now that has gone. All that is required is the ability to press the right buttons. Why does this matter? Perhaps it does not matter very much. But there is a certain amount of satisfaction to be gained from doing arithmetic and getting it right; one has achieved something, and achievement is an important ingredient in the quality of life. There is of course another side to the example used. Perhaps more important than skill at arithmetic is a shop assistant's knowledge of the products sold and skill in relating to customers. This is of course true, and undoubtedly the exercise of these skills gives satisfaction, but that does not alter the fact that *one* avenue of job satisfaction is gone. Another example concerns a highly skilled group, airline pilots. It has been suggested recently that airline pilots, who much of the time fly with the help of computing equipment, perform less well in emergencies due to a comparative lack of experience in flying the planes themselves (Dorsett 1994: 154). Their working lives have been described as "ninety-nine percent boredom and one percent terror"! It would not be surprising if there were less satisfaction to be found in looking at instrument panels than in exercising the skills in actually controlling airplanes.

We do not want to give the impression that with the introduction of computer technology work always becomes less fulfilling. We have already said that some boring and dangerous jobs are eliminated, and more of a positive nature will be said later. First, however, we want to consider perceptual skills and how this technology can affect them. Skills take time to develop, which presumably is one reason why we are proud of and derive satisfaction from them. Many jobs require motor skills or intellectual skills or skills in the perception of the physical world. A wine maker must develop the skill to recognise different tastes and smells in wine. A plasterer must be able to see small blemishes in walls. A wool classer must be able to notice differences in fleeces, and so on. But we do not merely grow up perceiving the world as it is. What we experience depends to some extent on our culture as well as on what skills we have developed. How it depends on our culture can be seen if we look briefly at the role of language. The basic point is that there is a close relationship between language, concepts, and perception. It is sometimes claimed that reality is relative to language—there is no absolute reality. There is only "your" reality, which is relative to "your" language. This is a bit strong, but it does contain a grain of truth. Our language is closely related to our concepts. Learning a new concept usually involves learning new words, or new meanings for old words, or learning to use old words in new ways. Conversely, learning new words or new uses for old ones, usually involves learning new concepts. And the concepts that we possess affect our perceptions. Consider the case of learning to taste the various subtleties of wine. Most of us just do not taste what an experienced wine taster does. However, with teaching and experience we can learn to recognise various flavours that we had not noticed before. As we learn this, we acquire concepts and language with which to describe them. Frequently, before we can taste something new, someone must point out to us, usually in language, that there is something there for us to taste. Once we are aware that there is something to look for, we look for it and quite often find it. When we do, our experience is to that extent richer. We experience more of reality than we did before.

What does this have to do with work and computer ethics? The essential point is that we must learn to perceive the world around us just as we must learn other skills, something that in most cases happens without our being aware of it. Sometimes, however, as in the wine example, we *are* aware. If we can learn to perceive something, we can also *not* so learn. Most of us, for example, could not put wool in the various classes that wool merchants would want. This is not only because we do not know what these classes are, but also because we would just not see the relevant aspects of the fleeces *now*. Some uses of computers have the potential to hinder such learning, and so to reduce the perceptual skills of humans. A photographer, for example, has lamented the fact that the constant use of light meters lessens the ability of photographers to accurately assess light conditions simply by looking (Goranzon 1988: 14). Not only do photographers not need to learn to assess light by looking, but those who had the skill are losing it. Without frequent use, skills die. A light meter is not a computer, but the point is the same. Expert systems, computer systems that simulate the behaviour of experts in a particular field, can sometimes perform as well as the expert, thereby making the expert, or the learning of that expertise by a human, less important. Is something important here being lost?

Skills are regularly lost as they become irrelevant to everyday living. Few people today have the skills required to win a Roman chariot race or even to build a haystack, but this is only slightly lamented. We do not even seem to worry too much about losing the ability to do rapid and accurate calculations in our heads. After all, why bother when calculators are inexpensive and readily available? However, there seems to be a relevant difference between these skills and perceptual ones. While life is richer the more we can do, perceptual abilities allow us to operate in a richer world, adding to our quality of life. It is the acquisition and development of these abilities that certain computer uses can inhibit, in the same way that a light meter can.

The moral question that arises here is whether computer systems should be used if they lessen human experience, thereby making that experience a little less rich. The obvious reply is that they should be used if they bring benefits, and this is plausible. But what is central is that this is seen as a *moral* issue, to be discussed case by case. The mere fact that some computer system can bring greater efficiency and higher profits does not mean that it is necessarily a good thing, if experience in general becomes poorer. "Life is more than meat, and the body more than raiment" (Luke 12:23). In cases in which perceptual skills are lost, perhaps those responsible for the introduction of the system have a moral obligation to introduce other activities that compensate for the resulting loss. Or perhaps the responsibility lies with the whole society. We will shortly argue that we, both as a society and as employers, do have such a moral responsibility.

Creation of New Jobs and Skills

The computerphile might by now be irritated. Of course computer technology makes some jobs and skills obsolete, but it creates others, the response will be. This is true, and we have no inclination to deny it. Many new and interesting types of employment are now available. Highly skilled computer programmers, systems analysts and designers, database managers, network specialists, and so on are now in demand. New skills are replacing old ones. These activities can all be highly satisfying and can contribute to the quality of life of the person possessing those particular skills. Solving a programming problem can be just as satisfying as solving a mathematical problem. Designing an attractive and functional user interface for a system has the same satisfaction as designing any successful artefact. So while we might mourn the passing of some jobs and skills, we welcome the birth of others.

Telecommuting

The place of work has also been affected by computer technology, especially because of the communication that that technology makes possible. It is now possible, in many fields of work, to do that work, or much of it, from home or anywhere else one likes. This telecommuting has advantages. It cuts the amount of time and money spent travelling to and from work, and helps to reduce pollution and other problems caused by traffic. It gives many people looking after young children or the elderly, the elderly themselves, or those with disabilities, the opportunity to enter or to stay in the workforce. It reduces the cost of office space for employers, allowing the price of goods and services to be reduced or the quality improved or profits to increase. These benefits should not be underestimated. They can undoubtedly add to the quality of life of some, particularly those who otherwise would not be able to have paid employment. But there are costs that should not be underestimated either. Most people like contact with others, and not just through a series of computers. We are basically social creatures, and most work environments are social. Telecommuting can cut off important avenues of social interaction. There may be little company for a morning cup of coffee or a drink after work unless there are others at home in your community, perhaps other telecommuters, with whom to socialise. The importance of these encounters with fellow human beings is considerable. Another concern is the exploitation of workers. Telecommuting facilitates this exploitation in two ways: First, workers are often contracted to do specific tasks, and so have no job security; and second, it is more difficult for people working in geographically disparate places to organise themselves to oppose exploitation. Not everyone of course will see these two factors as problems, but nevertheless for the workers involved they can be. Telecommuting is not necessarily a cause of exploitation if it occurs, but it does create a situation in which it can easily arise (see Snizek 1995 for a good discussion of some of these issues).

SOME CONCLUSIONS

We have considered some effects of computer technology on our working lives in three areas: number of jobs, types of skills, and telecommuting. Our discussions were intentionally general, because we are interested here in general principles that guide our actions and policies in the introduction and use of that technology in the workplace. While there are undoubtedly positive consequences, some of which have already been mentioned, the negative ones need to be highlighted because it is these that must be addressed. The negative consequences considered here were loss of jobs, loss of skills, lessening of human contact, and possible exploitation.

The question now is whether anyone has a moral responsibility to do anything about these problems, and if so who? It might be claimed that there are victims when any new technology is introduced. There certainly were in the Industrial Revolution! This might be unfortunate, but it is the price of progress. But this does not seem a satisfactory response. We will argue that there is a responsibility to assist those victims of change and that the responsibility lies with those who gain by the changes. Employers gain, so they have a responsibility, and so does society as a whole in many cases, with benefits mentioned before, such as lower prices for goods and services. There is a role for society too, to compensate.

How can the claim that something ought to be done be justified? Is it just an assertion? We will argue that there are good reasons for it. One reason is a utilitarian one. Putting people out of work, or forcing them into less rewarding jobs, creates social problems. The unemployed, in any civilised country, get some sort of benefit from the state in the form of payments, concessions, and so on. The more of these people there are, the greater the strain on the social security system. More important than this, however, is the link between unemployment and crime, particularly among the young unemployed. This again adds to the state's expenditure, in the form of extra funding for police forces and jails. It adds to living costs of employed individuals too, who need to spend more on security for their homes and other property, and it certainly increases anxiety. Being bashed or robbed is not on the list of most people's pleasures. From a utilitarian point of view, then, creating a disillusioned and poor class is not a good thing even if it does serve the interests of a few of the wealthy.

There is also a reason that does not fit so clearly into a utilitarian outlook. In many cases we do not think it justifiable to harm an individual, even if we thereby benefit others. Most people would think it wrong to kidnap a person and remove his kidneys to save the lives of two people who are desperate for a transplant, even though the action would mean a net saving of one life. And we do not think that the trauma and misery suffered by a gang-rape victim is justified by the pleasure of the rapists, no matter how many of them there are and how great their pleasure. In fact, we may well say that the greater their pleasure, the worse the whole situation becomes. The sort of case we are dealing with here is not of course comparable to either of these, but the point is that causing certain harms to individuals cannot be justified simply by greater benefits accruing to others. Harm is caused to those displaced by computers and this cannot be justified merely because others earn higher profits or can buy cheaper goods.

This not an argument against computers. Rather, in an affluent and flexible modern society, it seems unnecessary that those who are displaced should be harmed. If society had the will, alternative arrangements could be made so that other satisfying work could be found. This does not necessarily mean taking each displaced person by the hand and finding him or her another job, but it may suggest that governments should bear the above points in mind in exerting various influences on the labour market by means of such measures as taxation, employer incentives, and subsidies for retraining programmes.

Arguments have only been sketched here for the view that something ought to be done for those adversely affected by the introduction of computer technology. Much more needs to be said in order to make the case convincing, but we have tried to show how one can plausibly argue for it.

SUMMARY

In this chapter we have talked about the quality of life, and tried to make the notion of "the good life" at least precise enough for something useful to be said about computers and work. It has been argued that some people are inhibited from achieving a good life because of the introduction of computer technology into their workplace, and that both employers and society at large have some moral obligation to do something for them.

REFERENCES

ACM Code of Ethics and Professional Conduct 1992 (Draft). 1992. *Communications of the ACM* 35 (May): 94–99.

ACS Code of Ethics 1993. In electronic format. *IT Practitioner's Handbook*. Darling-hurst, NSW: Australian Computer Society.

Aristotle. *The Nicomachean Ethics*; edition of Thomson, 1971.

Clement, Andrew. 1994. Computing at work: Empowering action by "low-level users." *Communications of the ACM* 37 (January): 53–63.

Dorsett, Robert D. 1994. Risks in Aviation, Part 1. *Communications of the ACM* 37 (January): 154.

Forester, Tom, and Perry Morrison. 1995. *Computer Ethics: Cautionary Tales and Ethical Dilemmas in Computing*. 2d ed. Cambridge, MA: MIT Press.

Goranzon, B. 1988. The practice of the use of computers. A paradoxical encounter between different traditions of knowledge. In *Knowledge, Skill and Artificial Intelligence*, ed. Bo Goranzon and Ingela Josefson. London: Springer-Verlag, pp. 9–18.

Leinfuss, Emily. 1995. Marketing myths. *Information Age* [Melbourne, Australia] (July): 16.

Mill, John Stuart. 1863. *Utilitarianism*; edition of Sokar Piest, 1957.

Panteli, Nick, and Martin Corbett. 1995. Deskilling (1974–1994): 20 years after—in the era of empowerment. *Ethicomp 95: An International Conference on the Ethical Issues of Using Information Technology. Proceedings*. Vol. 1, unpaginated.

Snizek, William E. 1995. Virtual offices: Some neglected considerations. *Communications of the ACM* 38 (September): 15–17.

FURTHER READING

Brass, Charles. 1995. Virtual spirituality. *Information Age* [Melbourne, Australia] (September): 50.

Grosch, Herb. 1994. Dehumanization in the workplace. *Communications of the ACM* 37 (November): 122.

Talbott, Stephen L. 1995. *The Future Does Not Compute: Transcending the Machines in Our Midst.* Sebastopol, CA: O'Reilly & Associates.

10

Virtual Reality

Virtual reality is neither frivolous nor necessarily the most important invention since transistors. (Pratt et al. 1995: 17)

In the computing world there has long been talk of the virtual. "Virtual machines" and "virtual memory" have been around for decades. These are essentially technical terms of little interest to anyone outside the computing profession. More recently we have begun to hear of virtual libraries, virtual conferences, virtual offices, and even virtual villages and communities. These have all resulted from the spread of the Internet and of so-called "cyberspace." People do not need to attend a conference physically. They can instead communicate via the Internet. Rather than commuting to a physical office, workers can telecommute, that is, work from home via a computer link to an "office." Libraries, instead of being collections of books, journals, and the like in buildings, can consist of electronically stored documents accessible remotely by computer.

These cases of the virtual do not really constitute virtual reality, although they do, to a greater or lesser extent, simulate parts of reality. A virtual machine much of the time gives the impression of being a stand-alone computer (in one use of "virtual machine"), and a virtual library performs the central functions of a "real" library, such as the storage of documents and methods for their retrieval. With virtual reality (VR) however, there is a more total involvement with the computer-generated and -maintained environment. According to Pratt et al., VR is:

> an application that lets users navigate and interact with a three-dimensional, computer-generated (and computer-maintained) environment in real time. This type of system has three major elements: interaction, 3D graphics, and immersion. (1995: 17)

They go on to explain this:

> 3D graphics, a form of computer output, let users "see" the virtual environment. Immersion refers to the user's feelings of "presence" in the virtual world. An immersive application convinces users that they are in a replicated environment.

This is pretty much a description of the current state of the art, concentrating as it does on the visual. In the future, however, more of the senses will probably become involved. By donning special equipment linking you via sensory interfaces to a computer, you may enter a world of VR. Depending on the program and in some cases on technological advances and refinements, you may then have the experience of climbing Mt. Everest, of making a century at Lord's, or of making love, without these things actually happening: you are not really climbing or cricketing or copulating, it just seems that you are.

What, if any, moral issues arise from the virtual in general, and from VR in particular? There is nothing of moral interest in virtual machines or memory. The next level, however, does raise some concerns, but ones considered elsewhere in this book. For example, intellectual ownership is a much discussed topic in relation to virtual (or digital) libraries, and we considered this in chapter 5. Again, there is the question of whether important human interaction is threatened by telecommuting, virtual libraries, shopping and banking over the Internet, and so on. This issue was also raised in chapters 8 and 9. The uses of VR itself range from education to entertainment, from science to sex. Its scientific and educational uses are largely ethically uncontroversial, but some of its other uses are much less so. One of the best-known uses of VR is flight simulation, but there is an increasing number of others, for example, in surgery, in the treatment of the fear of heights, and in driving instruction (see Goble et al. 1995; Hodges et al. 1995; Kuhl et al. 1995). In all of these cases it would appear that behaviour in the real world can be enhanced by these virtual environments. Useful skills can be learnt without danger to the participants or to others in ways not previously possible, and this is surely uncontroversially good. At the other end of the spectrum are things not so obviously good: virtual murder, rape and other violence, and other kinds of sex. Virtual violence, including murder and rape, may have some redeeming features. If it could be shown that people committing those virtual crimes were less likely to commit the real ones, then there would be some argument for those uses of VR. While society would undoubtedly be better off without any violence, presumably virtual violence is the lesser of two evils. It is an empirical matter whether virtual violence would increase or decrease real violence, and given that there is still no consensus on the effect of television violence, any strong evidence of the effect of virtual violence is some way off. Virtual sex is another matter, and it is on this that we will concentrate in this chapter for two reasons. First, it is controversial, and second, it highlights an important question: Is the real better than the virtual? Is an experience of the real better than an experience of the virtual? Whether VR should be employed to train pilots and car drivers is hardly a moral issue, nor is its use in, for example, giving the physically disabled the "experience" of hiking through the Andes. Enriching people's experience is one way to enhance the quality of their lives. Some uses of VR obviously have this potential, enabling valuable experiences that could not be obtained in any other way. But perhaps virtual sex is not in this category and instead lessens the quality of life. Perhaps again, all virtual experiences are like this.

Real virtual reality is not quite with us yet, but aspects of it are, and it will undoubtedly be developed further. But suppose that it is all with us now, and choices must be made and counsel given about its acceptable uses. Or suppose that it is about to be with us, and we have the opportunity to help to decide whether it will be or not; it is often lamented that certain technologies, notably in the biomedical area, have raced ahead of our moral, social, and political readiness for them, and so let us suppose that here we have the chance to be ready and to allow or disallow the technology to exist.

VIRTUAL SEX

VR authority Howard Rheingold invites us to imagine dressing for a hot night in the virtual village. You don a lightweight bodysuit,

> something like a body stocking, but with the kind of intimate snugness of a condom. Embedded in the inner surface of the suit, using a technology that does not yet exist, is an array of intelligent sensor-effectors—a mesh of tiny tactile detectors coupled to vibrators of varying degrees of hardness, hundreds of them per square inch, that can receive and transmit a realistic sense of tactile presence. (1991: 346)

They receive and transmit by exerting counterforces against your skin, counterforces corresponding to those you would encounter when handling actual objects. "You can run your cheek over (virtual) satin, and feel the difference when you encounter (virtual) flesh. Or you can gently squeeze something soft and pliable and feel it stiffen under your touch" (1991: 346). By plugging your whole sound-sight-touch telepresence system (which will include 3-dimensional glasses and an appropriate auditory interface) into the telephone network, and "depending on what numbers you dial and which passwords you know and what you are willing to pay (or trade or do), you can find one partner, a dozen, a thousand, in various cyberspaces" (1991: 346); your physical body may be thousands of miles from your partner's, but you may touch and caress each other's virtual body.

> You will whisper in your partner's ear, feel your partner's breath on your neck. You run your hand over your partner's clavicle, and 6000 miles away, an array of effectors are triggered, in just the right sequence, at just the right frequency, to convey the touch exactly the way you wish it to be conveyed. If you don't like the way the encounter is going, or someone requires your presence in physical reality, you can turn it all off by flicking a switch and taking off your virtual birthday suit. (1991: 346)

Rheingold goes on to say, however, and no doubt to the disappointment of some, that the required technology seems to be a long way off. Extensive fibreoptic networks will be required, though we will eventually be getting them anyway. The mesh of transducers, the tiny, high-speed, safe but powerful sensor-effectors—"smart skin"—will take some time to develop. But the biggest problem, he says, and the one that puts the above scenario into the early-to-mid-twenty-first century rather than the 1990s, is that extremely powerful computers will be needed to make the enormous number of calculations required to monitor and control hundreds of thousands of sensors and effectors. "Every nook and protuberance, every plane and valley and knob of your body's surface, will require its own processor" (1991: 347). Suitably sophisticated olfactory and gustatory sensors and effectors, to complete the range of sensory communication, would presumably be technically challenging too. We shall just have to be patient.

Note that in Rheingold's scenario one is paying or trading or doing something in exchange for the experience; probably, in fact, one would be paying. So we have not only virtual sex, but virtual prostitution. And certain further concerns might arise on the strength of this. Before we tackle those, let us take Rheingold's scenario one large step further. Imagine that the virtual body you are virtually caressing is not a representation of an actual person who is virtually in contact with a similar representation of your actual body, but a virtual body behaving as it does merely as a result of a very sophisticated computer program, written or chosen presumably according to your wishes. There is no person on the other end, or at least no person having the sensation of contact with your body corresponding to your sensation of contact with hers or his. We have no idea when such a program and thus such an event might come about, but they seem imaginable. And if and when they do, they will provide virtual sex of a different kind: Your virtual partner will be animated not in a symmetrical way by someone who is doing essentially what you are doing, but in an asymmetrical way by the programmers and technicians who are not doing what you are doing at all. Let us distinguish these two kinds of virtual sex by calling them SV (for symmetrically virtual) and AV (for asymmetrically virtual) sex. SV sex so defined will not of course necessarily be symmetrical in any other way, as the partners may differ markedly in terms of motivation and enjoyment, just as in actual sex. In AV sex, the virtual partner may be more or less closely modelled (perhaps according to the client's request) on some real person, with any imaginable positive or negative degree of that person's approval or consent. But however close the modelling and however consenting the original person may be, it is appropriate to classify such a case as AV rather than SV, for the original is not having a reciprocal sexual experience, and may not even be alive at the time. Where the modelling is close and there is no consent, some may see it as a special case of rape; others may see it as morally distinguishable, without necessarily defending it.

Virtual Sex and Pornography

Virtual sex obviously invites comparisons with pornography. Various types of AV sex may be seen as respectively corresponding to various types of pornography: We may distinguish, for example, fiction or drawings of imaginary people on the one hand from drawings or paintings from life, photographs, and films on the other. And of course in the latter cases models may have been somehow exploited or otherwise harmed. Whatever the circumstances of its production, however, one of the standard objections to pornography is that it causes or may help to cause the consumer to commit sexual assaults, perhaps of the very kind that he (usually he) has enjoyed pornographically. Should there be a similar concern about either SV or AV sex? It is often pointed out that on such tricky matters we must be careful in drawing conclusions as to what causes what. Even if sexual offenders tend to be consumers of pornography, this does not show that the latter contributes causally to the offences even if the offenders say and believe that it does: The interest in pornography and the subsequent criminal behaviour may both be caused by some underlying personality factor absent in the many consumers who do not commit offences. Maybe so; but the would-be censor or opponent of pornography usually replies that it may at least act as a trigger, having an important causal role despite not being the most fundamental factor. And when virtual sex is available, may it not do so as well?

On the other hand, it is often claimed that pornography may actually serve as a "safety valve," by diverting or satisfying the lust of some potential rapists and molesters; it might be suggested that if virtual sex of either kind is realistic enough, it could do this job quite effectively. It may also seem that any virtual sex acting as such a safety valve is likely to be AV rather than SV, since not many women would wish to be "virtually raped" and not many children would wish to be, or would be allowed to be, "virtually molested." But some women may be prepared to take part in virtual rape, especially for money, just as some prostitutes presumably go along with some clients' rape fantasies and some actresses and models take part in simulated rape scenes; and some adults might, again especially for money, allow their virtual selves to be metamorphosed by VR technology into those of molestable children. Such SV safety valves may look very squalid, but they may be safety valves nonetheless. We should also consider the possibility that, to serve as a safety valve preventing a rape, an episode of either SV or AV sex need not be one of virtual rape; in at least some cases virtual consensual sex may do the trick. But this idea invites the reminder that many rapes, perhaps most of them, appear to be motivated primarily not by a desire for a sexual experience nor even by a desire to have actual sex, but by a desire to exercise power over an actual woman, power that in the rapist's view is most satisfactorily exercised in a sexual manner with or without additional violence. Where something like this is the rapist's motivation and he wants to exercise this power rather than merely experience the feeling of exercising it, then of course no VR experience known to be such will do. Another potential offender who will not be diverted by a VR safety valve is the one who, having experienced virtual sex (perhaps virtual rape), wishes to try out the real thing to see whether and how the two experiences differ, and is prepared to rape accordingly. As in the previous case, a high degree of sophistication and realism in the VR experience will not divert such a person, and here it may only encourage him. But of course he would have to be not only curious in this matter, but prepared to rape or otherwise assault someone to satisfy that curiosity. And it would seem difficult to be sure that the number of offences thus caused by the availability of VR sex would exceed the number prevented by its operation as a safety valve.

Someone who opposes indulgence in virtual sex or would wish to ban it may perhaps be confident of having good grounds for the belief that its bad consequences will outweigh its good ones. The bad ones may be thought to include not only criminal behaviour, but the treating of women and maybe children as sex objects, which pornography is often thought to help to cause. A hedonistic or Benthamite utilitarian, of course, would have to count the pleasures of the consumers among the good consequences; a wider view might count the sexual exploitation in some forms of AV sex as a bad thing, even where it causes no distress. Alternatively, one might hold that a significant *chance* of harm is enough to justify opposition or prohibition, even if this chance falls short of an even money bet. Such a position is vulnerable to a countermove in terms of a significant chance of *averting* harm by way of a safety valve, and also to the question of whether it can be established that the chance of harm is significant enough to justify the restriction of personal liberties, especially those of people whose other behaviour and personality give no cause for concern. But there is a different type of position that the opponent of virtual sex may take, along with or instead of either of the two just considered—the position that, quite apart from their consequences, virtual sexual experiences are in some way objectionable. How so? Two compatible answers may be offered.

First, it may be thought that such experiences—like various other sexual experiences including the enjoyment of pornography— are bad, and that it is wrong or sinful to seek them, because they contravene the purpose of sex as discoverable by biology or divine revelation or the "natural law." Sex is for procreation, it is said, and it is wrong to seek sexual experiences that do not at least leave that possibility open. But there are certain well-known difficulties here. Biology tells us only what actually happens in nature, not what we ought or ought not to do; divine revelation is hard to verify and (even in the most respected texts) not very explicit anyway on such matters as this, so that it requires interpretation by supposed authorities; and natural law, however understood, is not very obviously able to steer between one of these two problems and the other.

The Real and the Right

Alternatively, one may see virtual sex as a bad thing because it is essentially fake. The objection here does not specifically concern its sexual nature, but the fact that one is accepting or seeking a fake thing instead of a real one, a shadow instead of a substance, even if the shadow seems by courtesy of VR to be mighty substantial.

Several things may be said in response to this. First, in what sense is SV sex objectionably fake? Is the fact that the partners' sexual encounter is not directly body-to-body decisive, despite the fact that they are behaving symmetrically in our important sense, with each partner's sexual sensations being intentionally caused by appropriate behaviour of the other? AV sex may be a different matter, but it is not clear that SV sexual intercourse is any more fake intercourse than telephone conversation is fake conversation because the sound waves the talkers emit do not directly strike one another's eardrums, but rather are translated into and then out of electrical signals. But let us concede for the sake of argument that SV sex as well as AV sex should be seen as fake. Let us also concede that, other things being equal, a real X is better than—more worth having than—a fake X: The real Mona Lisa is more worth having than a forged Mona Lisa, real teeth are more worth having than false teeth, and so on. But what if the real thing is not available? If your real teeth have gone, you may well settle for a set of false ones, provided that the appearance and comfort are up to scratch, and nobody would think any less of you for that. What about the Mona Lisa? Here one might think that, rather than a fake that implausibly purports to be the original, it would be better to have what is obviously just a print; but a lot depends here on one's interests. A forgery might be of special charm or interest (or monetary value) because of its quality or who did it or owned it, while a print might be better to have for certain other purposes such as display in the school art room. Must the original, however, be preferable to either? Even if one could acquire the original by lifting it from the Louvre, one might very much prefer not to do so for various reasons: its safety, fear of arrest, the interests of would-be viewers, and so on.

Here, then, is a second important point: that while the real thing may be better to have than a fake or copy where other things are equal, other things may very well not be equal, as various considerations may affect one's overall preference. With respect to certain types of things, and in certain circumstances or for certain purposes, one may reasonably prefer to have a fake or copy of some kind rather than the real thing. One may choose to look at photos or films of exotic places rather than incur the trouble and expense (and maybe danger) of going there oneself; one may wear imitation fur for financial or moral reasons; one may eat imitation butter (margarine) for moral or health reasons. Why should someone not be prepared to make a similar choice, at least sometimes, as to sexual experiences? It is often noted that virtual sex, like currently available entertainments such as anonymous "fantasy phone calls," would be free of the risks of serious unwanted consequences such as pregnancy and disease. So some might be attracted to a form of sexual expression that, while inferior "in itself" to some more or less achievable alternative, is on balance preferable at least some of the time because it does not expose oneself or a partner to such risks. Particularly (though not necessarily) where one has the partner's interests in mind, one's preference here may actually be a moral one.

Quite apart from this there is a third important point to be noted. Even if any reasonable person would judge a certain choice to be inferior to some other, this does not mean that it would be morally wrong to make the former choice either occasionally or regularly. Eating at a fast-food restaurant may be thought inferior to dining in style at a slow-food one, but this does not mean that it is wrong to choose the former where one can afford the latter. We may be sad that someone makes the worse choice on some occasion or on most, and we may feel entitled or even obliged to say so. But this sentiment may well fall short of a judgement of wrongness; your regret at your friend's choice of partner or pastime may not amount to the feeling of blame or resentment, however mild, that is characteristic of judging something morally wrong. It would be a very demanding morality that extended judgements of obligation and wrongness to cover all such cases. And might one not see virtual sex—of either the SV or the AV kind—as a rather sad thing for a person to choose where the real thing is available, without seeing the choice as morally wrong?

Fourth, even if we do judge it morally wrong, this does not mean that we must favour any coercion or legal sanction. The proper province of the law may be seen as stopping short of prohibiting immorality as such: One may adhere to J. S. Mill's celebrated doctrine, which we came across in an earlier chapter, that we should have the liberty to do as we like "without impediment from our fellow-creatures, so long as what we do does not harm them, even though they should think our conduct foolish, perverse, or wrong." Unless it is argued that virtual sex causes or threatens to cause harm of some kind, such as mentioned earlier, to prohibit it would be an exercise of what is now called *legal moralism*, condemned by Mill and many others in the liberal tradition. The wrongness of a person's behaviour, says Mill, is, like folly, a good reason "for remonstrating with him, or reasoning with him, or persuading him, or entreating him, but not for compelling him, or visiting him with any evil in case he do otherwise" (1859: 11). The line between some forms of persuasion and some ways of "visiting with evil" may be rather fine, but Mill would certainly wish society to attempt to draw it in the case of behaviour that, even if widely thought to be wrong, cannot be plausibly seen as harmful to others. Various sexual activities such as homosexuality and promiscuity have been suggested as examples; virtual sex might be offered by some as another.

Virtual Prostitution

Both SV and AV sex will have their commercial manifestations. There will be SV prostitution, in which the real person on the other end may be regarded as akin to a prostitute, giving and having a sexual encounter for money. AV sex will presumably be typically commercial, and the technicians and marketers who arrange it will be akin to pimps. Cases will

include those in which the virtual partner is modelled on a fully consenting person who, if being paid, will thus have some similarity to the SV
prostitute, though one step further removed from the client; those in
which the virtual partner is modelled on a nonconsenting person who
would understandably see herself (usually herself) as being distastefully
exploited; and those in which the client's virtual partner is not modelled
on anyone in particular, so that there is a virtual prostitute but no real person who is virtually a prostitute.

Real prostitution, the sort familiar to human society as its oldest profession, is morally condemned on various grounds. As in the case of virtual
sex, the objections may be divided into two categories. On the one hand,
it is often claimed that prostitution is in some way harmful to one or more
of the parties directly or indirectly involved. Alternatively, or additionally,
it may be held that it is somehow a bad thing in itself, quite apart from
any harm it may do to anyone. Let us briefly consider these types of objection in turn and their bearing on virtual prostitution.

An important point often made is that much of the harm allegedly
caused by prostitution may be caused by factors involved in only some
types or instances of it, or by its being illegal or socially frowned on, not
by acts of prostitution as such. No doubt some prostitutes are exploited
in being coerced, or in pimps and clients taking advantage of their inability to keep themselves and their children in any other way. But could it be
said that even the up-market prostitute who prefers that occupation to a
more modestly paid but available alternative is being exploited, in a sense
substantial enough to mean that she is being wronged? To say that she is,
however strong her sense of free choice may be, is to suggest that no
woman could rationally and autonomously make that choice. There
seems to be no good reason to accept that suggestion, and good reason for
many prostitutes to be offended by it. The choice may not be one that we
ourselves would ever care to make, but the same goes for many a choice
that we would not dream of calling irrational.

SV prostitution could certainly be exploitative in very unpleasant
ways, although, given the hi-tech and possibly up-market nature of the
exercise, one may guess that the worst types of case would be found less
commonly there than in the real thing. And it could be just as nonex-
ploitative as the real thing too. AV cases of the kind in which the virtual
partner represents a recognisable, actual person could be very exploitative, either because that actual person has been subjected to unfair influence to be the model, or (perhaps more probably) because she has not
consented at all and the virtual prostitution consists in her virtual services being sold, not in her selling them. But where she has given her free
and informed consent, then she too (like her SV and actual counterparts)
can hardly be seen as exploited. And in AV cases of the more "fictional"

kind, in which the partner is not modelled on anyone in particular, there is nobody to *be* exploited.

According to moral objections of the second type, prostitution is simply wrong in itself. Why? It is hard to see why the selling of sex should be as such immoral, and, as often observed, hard to see how it differs morally from trading sex for other goods such as the material support and social status of a marriage, which some spouses more or less frankly do. Perhaps the wrongness of commercial sex, as well as much other sex, is seen as due to its lovelessness. It is not clear that it is *necessarily* loveless, at least on the part of the client, but let us agree that it is at least characteristically so. Well, what is wrong with loveless sex? Some have argued that just as sexless love may be perfectly all right, so may the converse: Love is a wonderful thing and so is sex and it is fine when the two coincide, but nothing is amiss when they do not unless someone is or may be hurt or betrayed, in which case the objection is not to the separation of love and sex per se but to the hurt or betrayal. It may well be that the idea of an entirely loveless sex life has little appeal for sensitive and loving people, but this does not mean that occasional loveless sex is unappealing to them too. Even if it is, more than the knowledge of this attitude would seem to be required to justify the claim that loveless sex is inferior. And there are several further points to be made that parallel those made earlier concerning the fake and the real. That which is inferior where other things are equal is not necessarily to be avoided where other things are not equal: What if embarking on a loving sexual relationship would create risks and harms for the other party? One might be about to go overseas for years, or off to war or a monastery. And of course in a given situation a loving relationship may simply not be in prospect. Next, to choose the inferior is not necessarily wrong; we may regret that someone chooses occasionally or exclusively to have loveless sex with prostitutes or casual pickups rather than developing a relationship in which the sex will be loving, but this is not the same as thinking it wrong. And finally, of course, even if we do think it wrong to have sex lovelessly and commercially, this is not to believe that it should be illegal. One might see prostitution as wrong but in essence harmless, and thus in that realm of private morality that is no business of the law. One might also see positive benefits in toleration, including the reduction of police corruption and other associated crime, and, as many have claimed, the protection of "honest women" from much molestation. One of us once met at a soirée a pleasant elderly lady who, commenting on a recent spate of sex crimes in a large city, said she thought there ought to be more brothels. "And they should be *free!*"

The day of the free brothel may be some way off; that of the virtual brothel may be a little closer. Perhaps the cost of the technology will eventually drop so much that the AV brothel is practically free anyway. Its commodity may fall somewhat short of an ideal many of us have about sexuality at its best, and in fact may be seen as multiply removed from that ideal in being fake, commercial, and loveless; but more than that is needed to justify moral condemnation, and more still to justify prohibition of its operation or of the development of its sensational technology.

VIRTUAL REALITY AND THE QUALITY OF LIFE

VR in general has the potential to enhance the quality of life, particularly in education and science; that is almost certain. Our argument about virtual sex suggests that this use of the technology too could make life more rewarding at least for some. Even if virtual sex is not as good and satisfying as the real thing in a loving relationship, it could nevertheless enhance the quality of life for those for whom a loving relationship is beyond reach, for whatever reason. It also has the potential for making life safer, especially for women and children, by providing sexual outlets that harm nobody. While the world would be a better place in all sorts of ways if everybody were in a loving relationship, this ideal world does not exist and almost certainly never will. We need therefore to use technology in ways that will make it a better place, even if not the best one. Although this chapter has concentrated on virtual sex and concluded that it does have a place, that is not really the main conclusion of the argument. The main conclusion is that, in general, there is nothing wrong with simulated or virtual environments. Virtual sex may not be as good (in some sense) as real sex, or virtual travel as real travel, but nothing follows from that about their rightness or wrongness. They may be a lot better than missing the experiences altogether. There are dangers of course. It would seem undesirable that someone should live his or her whole life in virtual reality if the real thing is available. Why it seems undesirable is not so easy to explain. Perhaps it is because living like this is parasitic on the rest of society. Another reason is that perhaps it is a denial of humanity. Such a person would go through life without facing and overcoming any challenges. But that is another issue. Our concern here has been to argue that there is nothing wrong with VR in itself, even for use in very personal areas.

SUMMARY

The discussion of VR has centred on virtual sex because it is controversial, and if VR can be defended here, it can probably be defended in almost any area. We argued that while it (virtual sex) might be poorer than the real thing, that in itself does not mean that it has no value. We found no arguments to support banning it, and it was suggested that it does have the potential to improve the quality of life for some. These arguments can be generalised to most applications of VR. It can improve our living, working, and playing environments.

REFERENCES

Goble, John C., Ken Hinckley, Randy Pausch, John W. Snell, and Neal F. Kassell. 1995. Two-handed spatial interface tools for neurosurgical planning. *Computer* 28 (July): 20–26.

Hodges, Larry F., Rob Kooper, Thomas C. Meyer, Barbara O. Rothbaum, Dan Opdyke, Johannes J. de Graaff, James S. Williford, and Max M. North. 1995. Virtual environments for treating the fear of heights. *Computer* 28 (July): 27–34.

Kuhl, Jon, Douglas Evans, Yiannis Papelis, Richard Romano, and Ginger Watson. 1995. The Iowa simulator: An immersive research environment. *Computer* 28 (July): 42–48.

Mill, John Stuart. 1859. *On Liberty*; page citations to edition of David Spitz, 1975.

Pratt, David R., Michael Zyda, and Kristen Kelleher. 1995. Virtual reality: In the mind of the beholder. *Computer* 28 (July): 17–18.

Rheingold, Howard. 1991. *Virtual Reality*. London: Secker & Warburg.

FURTHER READING

Antoff, Michael. 1993. Living in a virtual world. *Popular Science* (June): 124.

Communications of the ACM 38 (November) 1995. Special issue on digital libraries.

Communications of the ACM 39 (May) 1996. Special section on Virtual Reality.

Corliss, Richard. 1993. Virtual man! *Time* (November 1): 80–83.

Dvorak, John C. 1992. America, are you ready for simulated sex and virtual reality? *PC Computing* (May): 78.

Larijani, L. Casey. 1994. *The Virtual Reality Primer*. New York: McGraw Hill.

Pimentel, Ken, and Kevin Texeira. 1993. *Virtual Reality: Through the New Looking Glass*. New York: McGraw Hill.

Spring, Michael B. 1995. The virtual library. *Fantastic Futures: Virtual and in the Flesh*. National reference and information services conference, September 13–15. Presented by the Reference and Information Services Section of ALIA (RAISS).

Wexelblat, Alan, ed. 1993. *Virtual Reality: Applications and Explorations*. Boston: Academic Press Professional.

11

Minds, Machines, and Morality

> When a man *Reasoneth*, hee does nothing else but conceive a summe totall, from *Addition* of parcels: or conceive a Remainder, from *Substraction* of one summe from another. . . . Out of all which we may define, (that is to say determine,) what that is, which is meant by this word *Reason*, when wee reckon it amongst the Faculties of the mind. For REASON, in this sense, is nothing but *Reckoning* (that is, Adding and Subtracting) of the Consequences of generall names agreed upon, for the *marking* and *signifying* of our thoughts. (Hobbes 1651: 110–11)

The issues discussed in this book cluster around the idea of a computer as an information processing machine. We have looked at questions related to the processing and communication of information, and at some related to the information generated by computers. The environment, both real and virtual, created by various kinds of computer use was also examined. It remains now to consider the nature of the machines themselves. The *use* of these information processing machines raises a host of moral questions, some of which we have seen. Do the machines themselves raise any? Can they, in principle, be developed to a stage at which they should be treated as moral agents? This is one of those issues, mentioned at the beginning of the book, that has not arisen as a practical problem yet, but in all probability will, if there is continued research and development in intelligent machines. It is our contention that likely problems should be discussed, so that if or when they surface, we have some idea of how to deal with them. The central question here is whether or not computers can have minds as humans do, and it is to this that we now turn.

In previous chapters we looked at some ethical questions about computers performing tasks normally done by humans or that may indeed go well beyond the abilities of even the smartest humans. They perform feats of memory, of calculation, of deduction, and so on, that for speed and difficulty leave human minds far behind. Could computers themselves have minds? Could they reason as we do, going through a sequence of thought? Could they have any thoughts at all? What about feelings or emotions, such as irritation or anger or envy or love? When a system error occurs in my computer and it says "Sorry," it is behaving as if it is sorry. Nobody believes that it actually is, but could there be a computer that not only *says* "Sorry" but *is* sorry?

We shall approach this question by way of considering the nature of mentality in a human being. Each of us has this dimension of life, in that we think, feel, believe, and so on. What is the nature of this mentality? And what is its relationship to our physical body, and in particular to the brain, which clearly has a more intimate connection with our mentality than does the liver or the thorax? Many answers have been given to these questions, many different theories advanced on the "mind-body problem," as it is often called. We shall survey a few of these theories, inquiring in each case as to the compatibility of the theory with the idea of machine mentality.

THE MIND-BODY PROBLEM

Dualism

According to a very popular view, a human being has two fundamentally different components. One is the body, a physical thing with size, shape, mass, and so on, and including many physical parts and organs. The other is the mind, regarded as a nonphysical, immaterial thing, a thing without size or shape or mass but a thing nonetheless. The mind (or soul, as dualists sometimes call it) is the bearer or arena of our mentality, of our consciousness. Many dualists willingly concede that the mind and the body are closely linked, especially via the latter's brain; what goes on in the brain may have quite an effect on the mind, and vice versa. An injury to the brain, for example, or an encounter with alcohol, may produce odd perceptions in the mind, while a mental event such as a decision to go home will normally cause electrochemical events in the brain that in turn cause messages to go out to the muscles and the body to move in the direction of home or the means of getting there. But despite this causal interaction, intimate though it is, the mind and the body are different things. Many dualists hold further that they are not of equal importance in the constitution of a person—that your mind in fact constitutes the essential you. One of the most famous dualist philosophers, Rene Descartes, said in his Sixth Meditation, "I am really distinct from my body, and could exist without it" (Descartes 1642: 115). And like many other dualists, Descartes held that the mind (i.e., the person) does survive the body, and indeed survive it for ever. Dualism is consistent with many religious beliefs, and this helps to account for its popularity, though it also appeals to those who hope for survival of death in some form without any specifically religious focus. (Some people hope for life after death just so that they may see their loved ones again.) Yet it is important to be aware that the distinctness of mind and body is one question, the survival of the latter by the former is another, and survival forever is another one again. A bolt and its nut, though intimately related, are two distinct things that could survive apart; but it does not follow that either will survive forever, and they may even perish together by rusting away or melting. Nevertheless, dualism is obviously congenial to the ideas of life after death and immortality, and certainly more so than several other views we shall be mentioning.

Despite its appeal, dualism faces many problems for the reasons enumerated above and others. Essentially, a lot of the difficulties come down to one of the following: First, there is the problem of what sort of thing an immaterial mind or soul could be. It is tempting to try to define it negatively, by saying that it is invisible, intangible, and so on, but this fails to distinguish the mind from nothing at all, because *nothing* is also invisible, intangible, and so on. Positive descriptions of the mind, especially descriptions of what it is as distinct from what it does, are not easy to come by. Second, there is the problem of its relationship with the body, a relationship admitted by most dualists to be very close despite their utterly different natures. On the latter in particular Descartes was pressed by Princess Elizabeth of Bohemia, with whom he corresponded in later life, and was driven to say to her in exasperation that the union of soul and body is perfectly well understood until we come to do philosophy, and so perhaps we'd better not do too much philosophy—a rather startling suggestion from a man often called the Father of Modern Philosophy.

The difficulty of establishing the nature of an immaterial mind does not show that there is no such thing, and the difficulty of describing its relationship with the body does not show that there is none. If dualism of some sort is the correct view of human mentality, where does the computer stand? Surely, many say, a computer could not have an immaterial soul. How could the engineers at IBM or Apple possibly make and install one? Presumably they could not. But does it follow that a computer could not acquire a soul in some other way? When you mix concrete, you do not add the hardness as one of the ingredients like the cement and the sand and the water. The hardness comes about as a result of your mixing those three things together. Now admittedly the hardness is not a thing in the way that the dualist's mind or soul is supposed to be, but rather a quality, and a physical quality at that. Nevertheless, the example shows that in assembling X you can give it Y without doing so directly: Y may be a product of what you are doing directly. It may even be an unintended product, depending on the case. So, even though a computer builder could hardly make or take a soul and put it into a computer, could not a suitably sophisticated machine produce one for itself?

Many dualists will respond to this by saying that this is impossible, and that human bodies do not produce souls for themselves either. The soul is made by God and implanted by him at conception, according to the Catholic Church, at least since a ruling by Pope Pius IX in 1869; prior to that, the church accepted the ancient idea that "ensoulment" took place on the fortieth day of the pregnancy in the case of a male foetus and on the eightieth day in the case of a female one. But whenever it actually occurs, ensoulment is done by God, and he would never do it for anything nonhuman. He would certainly never do it for a machine. But why is this out of the question? How do we know what God might or might not choose to do? The soul, if it exists, is such a mysterious thing anyway, as is its relationship to the living body, as also are God's soul-making and soul-installing activities, that it seems highly presumptuous on our part to think we can be sure that he would never give one to a nonliving thing. Perhaps it would have to be sufficiently like us in some key respect, but who can know what that respect is or what degree of similarity would be sufficient?

Behaviourism

Let us now consider another significant view of mentality and its implications for computer mentality. Dualism is attractive to many people—especially those with a religious belief or an interest in an afterlife—but unattractive to others, who reject the idea of the body somehow containing and being directed by an immaterial mental substance, a "ghost in the machine." Among those who reject dualism are many psychologists of an empiricist temper—dealing only with, and believing only in, that which can be publicly observed, measured, and so on. The resident psychologist on a tabloid newspaper was once asked by a reader why he never said anything about the soul. He replied that he had looked up "soul" in his dictionary, and it said "the immaterial part of man." He then looked up "immaterial," and it said "irrelevant," so we need not bother with it. His reply traded of course on the ambiguity of "immaterial," but he may have been well aware of that.

Rejecting dualism, many psychologists and philosophers have embraced in one form or another a view known as behaviourism. Essentially, the behaviourist position is that there are not two things, the mind and the body, but only one, the body. Thanks largely to its brain but also of course to its nerves and muscles and bones and the rest, it behaves in all sorts of ways—walking, talking, leaping, weeping, and so on. Our mentality, says the behaviourist, is not something behind this bodily behaviour, a mysterious inner life that somehow directs it; rather, it just *is* our bodily behaviour in some way. To believe that today is Tuesday, for example, is to behave in a Tuesdayish way, which will involve responding appropriately to questions and doing other things one does only on Tuesdays; to be amused is to engage in amusement behaviour, such as laughing or smiling. The bodily behaviour is no doubt caused by neural and muscular events, with the brain playing an important role; but whatever its causes may be, mentality itself is constituted by the outward behaviour.

While dualism is commonly thought (perhaps wrongly, as we have seen) to exclude computer mentality, behaviourism seems to allow it, at least in principle. If a computer, or at least a computerised robot, could walk, talk, smile, and so on, then it would be displaying the behaviour of a being with mentality and so it would have to count, on the behaviourist view, as having mentality. Of course someone might say that a robot's smile is not a real smile, for a real one has to be on a human face and not on a metal or plastic one. But this would be to settle the issue against the robot simply by definition; it is not going to be allowed to qualify by displaying the appropriate behaviour, because the appropriate behaviour is by definition human. And a point scored against the robot in such a way is no point at all. We might just as well say that a robot could never be said to play the piano, no matter how beautiful the rendition of the Moonlight Sonata it produces by striking the keys with its metal fingers, because playing the piano is by definition an exclusively human activity.

So behaviourism, unprejudicially understood, seems to also allow the possibility in principle of machine mentality. How possible it is in practice will depend not only on technological developments but also on the level of sophistication in the behaviour required. Unfortunately, however, behaviourism seems very easy to refute. A mental state (such as feeling or believing something) cannot be in any way identical with the appropriate physical behaviour for the simple reason that it is quite possible to have either one without the other—a mental state without the physical behaviour in which it is normally expressed, or vice versa. Take, for example, amusement. This state may often or characteristically be manifested in certain outward behaviour, such as smiling or laughing. But you might feel amused without showing it at all—someone has committed a terrible *faux pas*, and tact or propriety require you to pretend not to have noticed. Or you might display amusement behaviour without being at all amused—your wealthy prospective father-in-law has just made a very feeble joke, and you fall about laughing. Another possibility is that you are acting in a play, and you have to laugh at something that amused you the first time you heard it but not any longer. The state of amusement then is something different from the amusement behaviour; they often occur together and are causally related, but in various circumstances either one may occur without the other. The same goes for other mental states—feelings, emotions, thoughts, beliefs. They are connected with our behaviour but distinct from it, and have an inner status.

A similar point may be made concerning computers. Outward behaviour is one thing, mentality is another. In his discussion of computer mentality, John Searle offers his now celebrated parable of the Chinese Room. Imagine, he says, that you are locked in a room with several baskets full of Chinese symbols (perhaps on pieces of paper). Further collections of symbols are passed into the room from time to time. You understand neither the symbols in the baskets nor the ones coming in, but you do have a rule book (in English) which gives you precise directions for responding to the incoming symbols by assembling ones from the baskets in certain ways and passing them out again. Unknown to you, the people outside the room call the collections they are sending in "questions" and the ones coming out from you "answers." If the rule book is good enough and you become quick enough, the answers you send out may be indistinguishable from those of a native Chinese speaker—but, says Searle, you are not learning any Chinese.

Following such rules then, no matter how well you do it, is not enough to give you an understanding of Chinese. You may acquire an excellent knowledge of Chinese syntax—the formal rules for arranging the symbols—but you have no semantics, for you do not know what the symbols mean. And when a computer follows the set of rules that constitute its program, then no matter how sophisticated that program and how excellent the machine's execution of it, this is not the same thing as having an understanding of what is going on, and thus not the same thing as having a mind. For, says Searle,

> There is more to having a mind than having formal or syntactical processes. Our internal mental states, by definition, have certain sorts of contents. If I am thinking about Kansas City or wishing that I had a cold beer to drink or wondering if there will be a fall in interest rates, in each case my mental state has a certain mental content in addition to whatever formal features it might have. That is, even if my thoughts occur to me in strings of symbols, there must be more to the thought than the abstract strings, because strings by themselves can't have any meaning. If my thoughts are to be about anything, then the strings must have a meaning which makes the thoughts about those things. In a word, the mind has more than a syntax, it has a semantics. (1984: 31)

And so, Searle concludes, "no computer program by itself is sufficient to give a system a mind. Programs, in short, are not minds, and they are not by themselves sufficient for having minds" (1984: 39).

Mind-Brain Materialism

If mentality is something inner—something causally connected with outward behaviour but distinct from it—then is the dualist view correct after all? Not necessarily. The dualist view is that the mind is an inner thing of an immaterial nature. But could it not be something of a material nature, namely the brain? According to a third view of the mind-body relationship, mental states such as belief or amusement are simply states of the brain, and mental processes such as inferring or speculating are simply processes in the brain. Mental goings-on are not just correlated with or connected with physical goings-on in the brain, as most dualists accept—rather, they *are* those brain goings-on. Such a view is sometimes called materialism, though this term is also used in a wider sense to cover any view to the effect that the only constituents of a human being are material ones. Behaviourism as defined above would count as a variety of materialism in this wider sense. The view we are now considering is certainly also materialistic in this wider sense, but differs from behaviourism in identifying our mentality with states and processes of the brain rather than with aspects or segments of outward behaviour. So we shall call it mind-brain materialism. Like other forms of materialism, it seems to rule out the possibility of life after death because the finish of your brain would be the finish of your mentality and of your personality and of you yourself—unless of course you see your survival in the continuance of the elementary particles that currently make up your body but will eventually make up other things. What they make up will depend on whether your body is burnt or devoured by worms or crocodiles or whatever. But our concern here is more with two other questions: (1) Does mind-brain materialism allow the possibility of machine mentality? (2) Is mind-brain materialism true?

To the first question, mind-brain materialists may not all give the same answer. Mental processes happen to be, on their view, brain processes; could they also occur in something that is not a brain but sufficiently like one? How similar would it have to be? Purifying blood is a process that takes place in the kidneys, but it may also occur in something that is not a kidney but relevantly and sufficiently similar to one – a dialysis machine; it does not occur in something which is like a kidney in other ways, such as a plastic kidney in one of those life-sized cutaway model bodies used in anatomy classes. Mental processes do not (presumably) occur in the model body's model brain. Could they occur in something sufficiently like a real brain, in whatever respects are relevant? And what are they?

Some will say that no computer could possibly be like a real brain in the relevant respects, for a very important one of those respects is that the latter is a living organ. Blood might be purified by a machine, either outside or inside the body, but mentality is something altogether different. It simply could not occur in anything that is not alive. Why not? With respect to dualism we wondered why a computer might not produce an immaterial soul or be given one by God; in the present case we might similarly wonder why a computer could not equal a brain in having mental processes. The supposed identity between mental and neural processes is a difficult thing to comprehend even in a human, and the defender of the possibility of machine mentality may ask why a similar identity could not hold between a mental process and an electronic one in a suitably sophisticated computer.

Now for our second question: Is mind-brain materialism actually true? It has the attraction for many people of giving a simpler account of human nature than the dualist's, while recognising (as the behaviourist does not) that there is an important difference between being in a certain mental state and behaving outwardly in the appropriate way. It also offers a neat explanation, which the dualist can hardly do, of the intimate connection between the brain and the mind. They are not two utterly different things, one with size and shape and mass and the other without, which are nevertheless mysteriously bound up with one another, "intermingled," as Descartes had to agree. Rather, they are one and the same thing. Somewhat similarly, what better explanation could there be of the intimate connection between the lives of Clark Kent and Superman than that they are one and the same person?

Despite its attractions, this version of materialism comes up against some important objections, of which we shall raise two. First, there is what is often called the Privacy Objection. It is said that there is a fundamental difference between what goes on in the brain and what goes on in the mind, which shows that they cannot be identical. The states and processes of your brain are, just like any other bodily states and processes, publicly observable, at least in principle. This means that other people may observe them as well as you can. There may well be portions or features of your body that you do not display in public for one reason or another, but others could observe them in principle; in fact some parts of your body can be observed more directly by others than by yourself, such as your eyes, for which you need a mirror, or the back of your head, for which you need two. Your brain and the events in it may never in fact have been observed by anyone at all, but, to whatever extent they could be observed by you, they could be observed equally well (and again, more directly) by others.

In contrast, consider some item in your consciousness—say a pain. Can other people "observe" or experience this pain of yours? They may well infer that you are in pain from your behaviour, including your linguistic behaviour; if you say "I am in pain," then we would normally infer that you are. Or we might infer that you are in pain from seeing what has just happened to you. A brick has just fallen on your unprotected foot; although you have not flinched or cried out, it is a fair bet that you are in considerable pain. But inferring that you are in pain, however reasonable the inference, is not the same thing as experiencing your pain in the way that you do. Even if neurophysiology develops to the point where the expert can say that such-and-such a brain process is associated with a sharp pain in the left knee, and that since that process is going on right now then you no doubt have such a pain in your left knee, that expert is still only inferring the existence of the pain. To experience your pain in the way that you do, one would have to have it—and who could possibly have your pain but you? It is said that some twins, or friends or partners, are so close to each other that when one is hurt or in trouble the other (who may be miles away) "feels it"; some men, apparently, feel labour pains when their partners are giving birth. Is such a man, who of course is not himself in labour, feeling someone else's pain, namely his partner's? Not at all. He is feeling only his own pain, even if it is caused in some strange way by hers, or by the physical events in her body, rather than by any obstetric events in his. Thus, it is held, physical things and events are, at least in principle, publicly observable, whereas mental items and events are essentially private. They are private in the sense that only the "owner" of a mental item can experience it directly, or experience it at all. And this essential difference between the mental and the physical shows that mind-brain materialism cannot be true.

A second important objection, which we shall discuss only briefly, is sometimes called the Infallibility Objection. Suppose you believe that your body is in a certain state—for example, that you have a cut on your hand. This belief of yours, strong though it may be, could conceivably be mistaken: you may be hallucinating, or the "blood" you see may be red dye that someone has spilt on you. There may well be circumstances in which it seems very far-fetched to suppose that such a belief could be mistaken, but it is at least conceivable, and so your belief is said to be fallible. In contrast, take your belief that you are in pain. Could you possibly be wrong about this? What would you think if the physiologist said that he or she had inspected your brain thoroughly, and there is no pain process going on, and so you cannot really be in pain? Would you accept this authority's judgement, and concede that you were wrong? Not at all. You would rightly insist that you are the authority on the question of whether you have a pain. Your belief, that is to say, is infallible. This is not to deny that you could be mistaken as to the *source* of your pain. You might complain of a pain in your right foot, for example, and have to be told that in fact you do not have a right foot at all, but have lost it, and are suffering from the "phantom limb" phenomenon in which the nerves that would normally carry the appropriate messages from the foot are being "triggered" somewhere further up the system. It may be too that there are other mental states with respect to which one is not infallible. Being in love is sometimes offered as an example. Could you be mistaken about being in love? How? But at least with respect to some mental states, such as being in pain or experiencing pleasure, it is held that your belief that you are in such a state is infallible. And so, it is concluded, here is a second difference between physical states and at least some mental states, which is another body blow, so to speak, to mind-brain materialism.

Functionalism

The last of the theories we shall introduce, and the newest of them, is one that appeals to many people sympathetic to the idea of machine mentality. Mentality, it is said, consists in certain causal powers possessed by certain things, such as brains, in certain states. A given state of the brain may cause certain things to happen, and another state may cause certain other things to happen; these states are mental states in virtue of the kinds of thing they cause, and they are different mental states (or mental states of different kinds) in virtue of the different kinds of thing they cause. Mental states are defined and classified by what they do, by their functions.

Two important questions arise. First, of what general type, or types, are the functions concerned? Many things have functional states that are not mental states; a lawnmower, for example, has states that together cause the lawn to be mown (engine running, blades attached, mower moving across lawn, etc.) but are not mental states. So what types of function count, for mentality? Second, could anything other than a brain have states that serve the appropriate functions?

On the first question, functionalists differ considerably among themselves. Some specify the functions in terms of outward behaviour—a given mental state is a state that produces certain behaviour of a kind we normally associate with that mental state. The state of amusement, for example, is one that produces amusement behaviour such as smiling or laughing. But this runs into the problems we encountered with behaviourism: In some cases there is amusement without amusement behaviour, or vice versa, and the same goes for many other states such as pain, fear, anger, belief, and so on. This makes it very difficult to define mental states of particular kinds in terms of what they do; they do not always do it, and other states do it too. Other functionalists seek to solve this problem by saying that the functions in question may include the causing of certain other mental states. So, for example, the mental state of amusement might be said to cause the desire to smile or laugh, as well as actual smiling or laughing. Such a move may cover the case of the person who is amused but does not show it—if we can suppose that he or she has at least a desire to smile or laugh, caused by being amused—but there is still the problem of the faker. When you laugh at the rich man's feeble joke you are not only laughing, but doing so because of a desire to laugh. Yet this desire has not been caused by amusement, but by some other mental state such as a desire to impress him. So we have not yet functionally differentiated the mental state of amusement from other mental states such as this.

Setting this problem aside, or supposing that it can be dealt with, an important thing to notice about the appeal to causing other mental states is that we are giving up hope of defining mental states in general. If we have to say that a certain mental state is one that causes certain other mental states, how much have we said about the nature of mental states as such? It seems rather like saying that a horse is something that produces other horses. Does this tell us much about what it is to be a horse? Some functionalists do not mind this too much, for they are more interested in establishing causal links among states of various specific kinds than in defining mentality in nonmentalistic terms. And much of the work they have done is very sophisticated and instructive in extending our understanding of mental operations and relationships. But let us now turn to question (2) above. Whatever the causal functions required for mentality or for any particular instance of it might be, could anything other than a brain fulfil them? Could a computer?

Functionalists differ as to whether anything other than a brain will in fact ever do so. But they agree on this: There is no reason in principle why a computer could not. It may require circuitry that copies that of the brain, and such sophisticated electronics may be a long way off, but it cannot be declared impossible. Some functionalists go further and say that even such brainlike physical circuitry may not be required, that even an immaterial substance like Descartes' mind could (conceivably) have such functions. The crucial thing for a functionalist is what a state can *do*, not what it is a state *of*. One point that seems to justify the functionalist's openness to the idea of things other than brains having mental states is that the nature of those states, and their relationship to physical states, are at best very mysterious indeed. As we have seen, it is not at all easy to define mental states in physical terms or any other terms, and the "reductionist" attempts by behaviourists and other materialists to show that they are nothing but behavioural dispositions, or brain states, run into serious problems. If the relationship between the material and the mental, the physical and the psychical, is impenetrably mysterious anyway, why should we narrow-mindedly rule out the possibility of such things occurring in computers or even indeed in immaterial spirits, should there be any? Immaterial spirits are somewhat elusive. But computers undoubtedly exist, and are undoubtedly becoming more and more sophisticated. What would a computer have to be like, what would it have to do, to satisfy us that it had mental states?

THE TURING TEST

Some people are of course so opposed to the whole idea of machine mentality that they would never concede its existence, no matter what a candidate computer was like or what it seemed able to do. The computer's supporter may suggest that such people are unimaginative, unable to conceive of a thinking and feeling being that is so very different in appearance and construction from ourselves. Or perhaps that they are prejudiced against the computer because they want to believe that only humans have mentality. Perhaps it is important to them to be able to see humans as different from, and thus superior to, everything else in this key respect; human dignity would suffer if we had to share it with anything else, especially an artefact. Or perhaps they are afraid of what might happen to us if computers or computerised robots develop mental states, which may well include desires to take over the world and enslave or exterminate us.

Reasons for hoping that computers cannot think or feel are not reasons for concluding that they cannot. Mindful of this point, and of the fact that many people do not appreciate it, many other people on both sides of the debate are keen to see computers, present and future, given a fair trial. The best-known suggestion is the Turing Test, named after its proposer, the pioneer computer scientist Alan Turing. Turing starts by asking what signs and signals we use to infer that other humans are thinking. It is clearly, he says, a matter of the kind of conversation we can have with them, and not a matter of their physical appearance. Therefore, let us test the computer according to its conversation, and in such a way as to prevent being prejudiced by other, irrelevant, features. We may do this by putting ourselves in a room with two computer terminals, each of which is connected to something outside the room: one is connected to a person of normal intellect and the other to a computer, but we do not know which way round. We now communicate with each of the latter, via our terminals, and try to determine which is the person and which is the computer. We may say or ask anything we like, but each respondent is allowed to lie to protect his/her/its identity, so it is no good asking, for example, "Are you the computer?" If the computer is so accomplished that we cannot tell the difference, then, says Turing, it has passed the test and should be credited with being a thinking machine. In his 1950 paper he expressed the belief that by the end of the century it would be possible to program computers to perform so well that an average interrogator would not have more than a 70 percent chance of making the correct identification after five minutes of questioning (Turing 1950: 442).

Here, many will say, is the problem. The computer, however impressive its performance, has to be programmed to do its stuff; it cannot achieve anything genuinely creative, which is the mark of mentality, and so a "pass" in the Turing Test is not sufficient to establish mentality. This objection, in one form or another, is commonly associated with the name of Lady Lovelace. Ada Lovelace, who was a daughter of Lord Byron, lived well before Turing and thus could not comment on his test, but she was an associate of the mathematician Charles Babbage who planned a computer called an "analytical engine" in the 1830s. Lady Lovelace said that the engine "has no pretensions to *originate* anything. It can do *whatever we know how to order it* to perform" (quoted by Turing 1950: 450; her italics). She did not say that no machine could ever be creative, or think, but her name is linked with the objection that the computer's need for programming excludes the possibility of mentality.

Three replies may be offered. In the first place, why does mentality have to be creative in any significant sense? Thoughts may be dull and routine but thoughts nonetheless, and the vast majority of human thoughts and ideas are surely just so. Imagine (or recall) a conversation with a very boring person; you may not doubt that there is thinking going on, though it lacks any originality or creativity. Similarly, if the computer lacks creativity it does not thereby lack mentality. Second, is it clear that a programmed computer cannot be creative? It may be true that it will do only what it is programmed to do, but this does not exclude the possibility of its doing things that are the consequences of its program without being envisaged by the programmer. Many years ago a computer with a geometry-theorem-proving program evidently produced a completely novel proof of a Euclidean theorem that the base angles of an isosceles triangle are equal by flipping the triangle through 180 degrees and declaring the original and its "flip" to be congruent (Evans 1992: 433). This proof was previously unknown to human geometers, who accorded it high praise.

Third, is it not possible that human creativity is due anyway to the "programming" we receive from hereditary and environmental sources? There may or may not have been any divine intention in the selection of the mix of factors that turned you out as you are. And there may or may not have been any human intention, with one or both of your parents choosing to mate in such a way as to produce a child of a certain stamp or raising you in an environment conducive to a desired outcome; most of us have been influenced by some parental choices at least of the latter kind, though such influencing is not as a rule nearly specific enough to be thought of as programming. But whatever the level of intention—divine or human—in the selection of your formative hereditary and environmental factors, your constitution and behaviour are thought by some people to be fully the products of those factors nonetheless, and that includes what we call our creativity. The works of Leonardo and Shakespeare and

Mozart resulted from ideas that had never been had (at least in those forms and combinations) before, but those ideas in those forms and combinations were still produced by what had gone before. And any being with enough comprehension of the relevant circumstances and laws of psychology and/or physiology and so on could have predicted those artistic productions (together with every other human thought and deed) in detail, and maybe somewhere such a being exists and did predict them. The actual level of our understanding seldom however permits more than rough predictability of some human behaviour, and so we are surprised and impressed when something new and undreamt of is produced.

The view of human nature just sketched is known as determinism. It is a highly controversial view, with some very challenging apparent implications for human dignity and moral responsibility, and around it there still rages a major and many-faceted philosophical debate. To enter that debate here would unfortunately take us well away from our present concern. We raise the topic not in any hope of resolving it, but to query further the Lady Lovelace challenge to the Turing Test. Any degree of creativity suggestive of mentality may, for all we know, be the result of "programming" in ourselves or in anything else. So the legitimacy of the Test seems to be upheld.

Another challenge, however, comes from John Searle. Remember his parable of the Chinese Room. With the right instructions in the room and enough practice, says Searle, he can fool native Chinese speakers; he can thus pass a test analogous to the Turing Test, but without understanding any Chinese. So, if the computer's performance could also be the result of very good instructions, that is, its program, its ability to pass the Turing Test no more proves its mentality than Searle's ability to fool the Chinese speakers proves that he understands Chinese (1980: 419). In response to this argument it is often said that, although the person in the room does not understand Chinese, the whole system does. The system includes the room, the baskets of symbols, and the ledgers giving the detailed instructions for Searle to follow, as well as Searle himself. And this system as a whole understands, or incorporates an understanding of, Chinese; how else could the instructions be so good as to enable Searle to fool the native speakers? Similarly, the computer system as a whole, including the hardware and the software, is what passes the Turing Test and therefore demonstrates understanding, that is, mentality.

Searle says that this reply is inadequate. Reminding us of his distinction between syntax and semantics—between following formal procedures, as he does in the Chinese Room when he follows the instructions, and attaching meanings to those procedures, which he cannot do—he says that syntax is not sufficient for semantics, and there is no way that the system can get from the former to the latter. And in this he seems to be quite right. But does it follow that the computer could not acquire the semantics in some other way? Between sessions in the Chinese Room, Searle might enroll for lessons in Chinese and begin to make sense of the messages he is handling in the room. Similarly, could the computer acquire mastery of the semantics in some way other than via its programmed mastery of the syntax?

How could it do this? Let us approach this question by imagining three artefacts, named Tom, Dick, and Harry. Tom, synthesised by a clever biochemist, is molecule-for-molecule indistinguishable from a human being. Searle imagines such an artefact, and says that he could presumably think, but is just a "surrogate human being" (1984: 36). Dick is a digital computer, with an impressive program that enables him to pass the Turing Test. This, on Searle's view, would not show that Dick can think. Harry differs from Tom and resembles Dick in being nonbiological, being made of silicon and plastic and so on. But he differs from Dick in having a brain that duplicates the neural structure of a human being; the neurons and the pathways and the rest are replicated electronically. Suppose that Harry then sails through the Turing Test, answering every question with flair, and lying, where necessary, through his silicon teeth. Could he have acquired semantics, as we do? Searle may be justified in refusing to accept Dick as a thinking computer. But what about Harry?

ROBOT RIGHTS

Many people's first reaction to the prospect of thinking computers will no doubt be one of fear. Will they take over the world? What will they do with us? Many a sci-fi scenario has exploited this fear, describing bizarre fates that may await the human species. Perhaps there will be specific AI projects that should be stopped or disallowed because of such risks; perhaps any attempt to build a thinking machine presents unacceptable risks, whatever the intentions of the builders and programmers might be. Let us suppose that it is too late to stop them, and we have before us Harry. Suppose too that there seems no reason to fear him (it?), or at any rate no reason to fear it any more than the average stranger you meet in the street. How should we treat it? The stranger in the street has various rights, many of which have implications for your conduct; you ought not, for example, rob or assault or kill him or her, and maybe you ought not to do certain things that he or she may find threatening or offensive. What about Harry? Does it have rights too? Rights to what?

Some of the particular rights possessed by a human seem hardly applicable to a computer. Not being alive it cannot be killed, and so it has no right not to be killed; and while it could be physically assaulted, it could not be sexually assaulted. But what if Harry has sexual organs as well as a "neural" structure that mimics the human one in such a way as to allow sexual trauma? As far as killing is concerned, it might be suggested that switching off the power supply to a thinking and feeling computer would stop it from thinking and feeling, and thus be tantamount to killing it. Or, since the power supply may be restored and with it the mental activity, would it be more like rendering a person unconscious? This of course would still be regarded as contravening the person's rights, unless of course it is a case of medical anaesthesia to which the patient or his or her representative has consented; and it may be not far removed from killing if the victim is rendered unconscious for a very long time. But even if some human rights are inapplicable in any form to a computer or robot, it does not follow that it has no rights at all. The right to secondary-level education is not applicable to people who are severely mentally retarded, but they have plenty of other rights.

The retarded person is at least human. Can something that is not human at all be said to have rights? People do talk of animals having rights, but can this really make sense? Animals cannot claim these supposed rights, nor are they seen as having moral responsibilities, and surely to have rights you must be able to claim them and you must have responsibilities too. Several replies to this may be offered. First, seriously retarded humans cannot claim their rights and cannot be seen as having moral responsibilities, but surely they have the right not to be killed and not to be exploited in various ways. Second, whatever we think about animals, who says that a suitably sophisticated computer like Harry could not claim rights or have responsibilities? Third, even if something cannot be said to have rights it may still be wrong to treat it in certain ways: It may be thought wrong, for example, to cut down a magnificent tree or demolish a beautiful building, and not only because people have a right to enjoy it. It has value, one might say, even if no rights. And perhaps this could apply to Harry, though the second reply seems more relevant.

At this point a rather different move might be made against Harry. Whatever its qualities and abilities might be, it is a human creation. And the creator of a thing has the right to do with it whatever he or she likes; if you build a house (out of your own materials) you are entitled to demolish it, unless you have contracted to sell it, and the same goes for anything else you make. So, while nobody else may have the right to destroy or "mistreat" the computer you have built, you may do what you like with it. In response to this we might say that parents, for example, who create children out of their own materials (eggs and sperm), do not thereby acquire the right to do what they like with them. A few people do think they have a right to kill their unwanted infants, and a lot of people used to think that it was quite in order to subject their young children to labour in chimneys or mines. Some people still treat their children as items of property, according them little respect as persons; but even if many of us now are sometimes guilty on this count, we recognise important limits on parents' rights over their children. Why should the same not apply to computer engineers' rights over their creations? It is true that parents do not design their children in the way that computer builders do; the procreative act may not in fact have been intended to be procreative at all. But this difference may be only one of degree. Some parents do try to design their children in certain ways, by choosing an appropriate coparent, adopting certain dietary and environmental habits during pregnancy, and so on; do they thereby acquire greater rights over the life of the child? If by genetic and/or environmental engineering they could have a child designed precisely to order, would they acquire greater rights still? Surely not. The child's potentialities and needs are the basis of important rights that severely restrict the rights of even its parents, whatever the extent to which the parents designed and made the child to be as it is.

There seems, then, no conclusive reason to deny appropriate rights, and the appropriate treatment, to a computer like Harry. We leave it to you to imagine what life with Harry might be like. We also leave you with this question. We may well have difficulty in believing that Harry really does have thoughts and feelings and therefore rights. He (no, it!) is only a machine, after all; it is not made of flesh and blood, but of silicon and plastic and so on. Can it really think and feel, however plausibly it claims to be able to? Many of us may well have a strong and lingering doubt. But given what is at stake—life, or something like it, liberty in an appropriate form, and the pursuit of electronic happiness—should we not give Harry the benefit of the doubt?

SUMMARY

In this chapter the question was examined of whether computers, or any machines, could be thinking and feeling things and therefore have moral rights. The discussion began with a consideration of the mind-body problem. There was an attempt to establish that no sound objections exist in principle to machines having minds. Turing's test for intelligence was then examined, and it was suggested that if any machine, or robot, could pass it, we should give it the benefit of the doubt and assume that it does have moral rights.

REFERENCES

Descartes, Rene. 1642. *Meditations on First Philosophy*; page citations to edition of Anscombe and Geach, 1971.

Evans, Christopher. 1992. Can a machine think? In *Philosophy and Contemporary Issues*. 6th ed. Ed. John R. Burr and Milton Goldinger. New York: Macmillan, pp. 423–35.

Hobbes, Thomas. 1651. *Leviathan*; page citations to the edition of Macpherson, 1975.

Searle, John R. 1980. Minds, brains, and programs. *The Behavioral and Brain Sciences* 3: 417–24.

Searle, John R. 1984. *Minds, Brains, and Science*. London: British Broadcasting Corporation.

Turing, A. M. 1950. Computing machinery and intelligence. *Mind* 59: 433–60.

FURTHER READING

Clarke, Roger. 1993. Asimov's laws of robotics: Implications for information technology, Part 1. *Computer* 26 (December): 53–61.

Clarke, Roger. 1994. Asimov's laws of robotics: Implications for information technology, Part 2. *Computer* 27 (January): 57–66.

Dreyfus, Hubert L. *What Computers Still Can't Do: A Critique of Artificial Intelligence*. Cambridge, MA: MIT Press.

Epstein, Robert. 1992. The quest for the thinking computer. *AI Magazine* 13 (Summer): 81–95.

Feigenbaum, Edward A. 1996. Turing award lecture: How the "What" became the "How." *Communications of the ACM* 39 (May): 97–104.

Haugeland, John. 1987. *Artificial Intelligence: The Very Idea*. Cambridge, MA: MIT Press.

Johnson-Laird, P. N. 1988. *The Computer and the Mind: An Introduction to Cognitive Science*. London: Fontana Press.

Matthews, Robert. 1994. Computers at the dawn of creativity. *New Scientist* 144 (10 December): 30–34.

Reddy Raj. 1996. Turing award lecture: To dream the impossible dream. *Communications of the ACM* 39 (May): 105–13.

Glossary

Absolutism—the view that actions of certain kinds are always right or always wrong.

Artificial intelligence—humanlike intelligence in machines or the discipline of attempting to develop it.

Behaviourism—the view that mental states and events may be understood or defined purely in terms of outward physical behaviour.

Bug—an error in a computer program.

Consequentialism—the normative view that the rightness or wrongness of actions is determined solely by their (likely) consequences. Utilitarianism is a type of consequentialism.

Determinism—the view that everything that happens (including all human thought and behaviour) is caused by what has gone before and is at least in principle predictable.

Diversity problem—in ethics, the problem (for objectivists) of explaining the diversity in moral beliefs.

Divine command theory—the objectivist theory that the right action is that which is commanded or approved by God.

Dualism—the view that the mind is an immaterial thing, distinct from the body even if causally related to it.

Functionalism—the view that mental states are to be understood in terms of their causal functions and that in principle things such as computers could have such states.

Greatest happiness principle—see Utilitarianism.

Hedonism—the normative ethical view that pleasure is the only thing good for its own sake.

Image manipulation—the alteration of images stored electronically, usually on a computer disk.

Internet—the network linking computers worldwide.

Intuitionism—a type of objectivism stating that we know moral truths by a special intellectual faculty, intuition.

LambdaMOO—the most famous MOO, and primarily the context for a game in which players take on personalities and interact in various ways with one another.

Meta-ethics—the study of the status or meaning of moral beliefs.

Mind-brain materialism—the view that mental states and events are identical to brain states and events.

MOO—a "place" or environment on the Internet where people can interact online. Currently MOOs are mainly used for game playing.

Naturalism—the meta-ethical view that morality may be defined in terms of ordinarily observable things and qualities, as opposed to supernatural ones.

Normative ethics—the study of particular moral questions, and of general principles and stances on how we ought to act.

Objectivism—the meta-ethical theory that there are objective moral truths independent of societies and individuals.

Other-regarding actions—actions that may (significantly) affect other people, as opposed to self-regarding actions.

Paternalism—restricting the liberty of someone for his or her own good.

Pluralism—the normative ethical view that our duties cannot be reduced to one fundamental principle.

Prolog—a computer programming language based on logic (Programming in Logic).

Relativism—the meta-ethical position that there are no objective moral truths. All moral beliefs are relative to, for example, a culture (cultural relativism) or the individual (subjectivism).

Self-regarding actions—see Other-regarding actions.

Subjectivism—the meta-ethical relativist position that moral beliefs are relative to the individual; for example, the view that moral judgements express the speaker's desires and aversions.

Turing Test—a suggested test for artificial intelligence in terms of the machine's ability to converse.

Utilitarianism—the normative ethical view, closely identified with Jeremy Bentham and J. S. Mill, that the right action is that which promotes the greatest happiness or pleasure for the greatest number of people affected.

Verification problem—in ethics, the problem of establishing the truth or falsity of supposedly objective moral judgements.

Bibliography

ACM Code of Ethics and Professional Conduct. 1992. [On-line]. Available gopher://
ACM.ORG:70/00%5Bthe_files.constitution%5Dbylaw17.txt

ACM Code of Ethics and Professional Conduct 1992 (Draft). Communications of the ACM
35 (May): 94–99.

ACS Code of Ethics. 1993. In electronic format. *IT Practitioner's Handbook.* Darling-
hurst, NSW: Australian Computer Society.

ALA Policy Manual, Section Two (Position and Public Policy Statements). 1996. 52.4
Confidentiality of Library Records. [On-line]. Available gopher://gopher.
ala.org:70/11/alagophviii

ALA Code of Ethics. 1995. [On-line]. Available gopher://gopher.ala.org:70/
00/alagophii/ethics.txt

ALA. Commission on Freedom and Equality of Access to Information. 1986. *Freedom and Equality of Access to Information: A Report to the American Library Association.* Chicago: ALA.

Alexandra, Andrew. 1996. Computer networks and copyright. In *Issues in Computer
Ethics.* Wagga Wagga: Keon Publications, pp. 1–11.

Alexandra, Andrew, and Seumas Miller. 1996. Needs, morals, self-consciousness, and
professional roles. *Professional Ethics: A Multidisciplinary Journal* (forthcoming).

American Library Association. 1989. *ALA Handbook of Organization 1989/90 and
Membership Directory.* Chicago: American Library Association.

Anderson, A. J. 1989. The FBI wants you—to spy. *Library Journal* (June 15): 37–39.

Anderson, Scott. 1993. *Morphing Magic.* Indianapolis, IN: Sams Publishing.

Anscombe, Elizabeth, and Peter Thomas Geach, ed. and trans. 1971. *Descartes:
Philosophical Writings.* London: Nelson.

Antoff, Michael. 1993. Living in a virtual world. *Popular Science* (June): 124.

Aristotle. *The Nicomachean Ethics*; edition of Thomson, 1971.

Australian Library and Information Association. 1992. *1991/1992 Handbook*. Canberra: Australian Library and Information Association.

Bass, Jeremy. 1995. In the belly of the beast. *Information Age* [Melbourne, Australia] (September): 36–40.

Bayles, Michael D. 1981. *Professional Ethics*. Belmont, CA: Wadsworth Publishing Company.

Benn, Stanley I. 1988. *A Theory of Freedom*. Cambridge: Cambridge University Press, chapters 14, 15.

Berlin, Isaiah. 1969. *Four Essays on Liberty*. London: Oxford University Press.

Boden, Margaret. 1987. *Artificial Intelligence and Natural Man*. 2d ed. New York: Basic Books.

Boden, Margaret. 1990. *The Creative Mind: Myths and Mechanisms*. London: Weidenfield and Nicolson.

Brass, Charles. 1995. Virtual spirituality. *Information Age* [Melbourne, Australia] (September): 50.

Burr, John R., and Milton Goldinger, eds. 1992. *Philosophy and Contemporary Issues*. 6th ed. New York: Macmillan.

Callahan, Joan C., ed. 1988. *Ethical Issues in Professional Life*. New York: Oxford University Press.

Callahan, Sean. 1993. Eye Tech. *Forbes ASAP* 151 (June): 57–67.

Clarke, Roger. 1993. Asimov's laws of robotics: Implications for information technology, Part 1. *Computer* 26 (December): 53-61.

Clarke, Roger. 1994. Asimov's laws of robotics: Implications for information technology, Part 2. *Computer* 27 (January): 57–66.

Clement, Andrew. 1994. Computing at work: Empowering action by "low-level users." *Communications of the ACM* 37 (January): 53–63.

Cole, Wendy. 1995. The Marquis de Cyberspace. *Time* 27 [Australia] (July 10): 53.

Collins, H. M. 1990. *Artificial Experts: Social Knowledge and Intelligent Machines*. Cambridge, MA: MIT Press.

Collins, W. Robert, Keith W. Miller, Bethany J. Speilman, and Phillip Wherry. 1994. How good is good enough: An ethical analysis of software construction and use. *Communications of the ACM* 37 (January): 81–91.

Communications of the ACM 38 (November) 1995. Special issue on digital libraries.

Communications of the ACM 39 (May) 1996. Special section on Virtual Reality.

Corliss, Richard. 1993. Virtual man! *Time* (November 1): 80–83.

Crevier, Daniel. 1993. *AI: The Tumultuous History of the Search for Artificial Intelligence*. New York: Basic Books.

Dejoie, Roy, George Fowler, and David Paradice. 1991. *Ethical Issues in Information Systems*. Boston: Boyd & Fraser.

Descartes, Rene. 1642. *Meditations on First Philosophy*; edition of Anscombe and Geach, 1971.

DIALOG. 1990. *Terms and Conditions. DIALOG Classroom Instruction Program*.

Dibbell, Julian. 1994. Data Rape: A Tale of Torture and Terrorism On-Line. *Good Weekend: The Age Magazine* [Melbourne, Australia] (19 February): 26–32.

Dickens, Charles. 1854. *Hard Times*; edition of Ford and Monod, 1966.

Dorsett, Robert D. 1994. Risks in Aviation, Part 1. *Communications of the ACM* 37 (January): 154.

Dreyfus, Hubert L. 1992. *What Computers* Still *Can't Do: A Critique of Artificial Intelligence*. Cambridge, MA: MIT Press.

Duguid, David. 1994. The morality of synthetic realism. Unpublished paper presented at a conference at Noosa Regional Gallery, Tewantin, Queensland, Australia, March.

Dvorak, John C. 1992. America, are you ready for simulated sex and virtual reality? *PC Computing* (May): 78.

Elmer-Dewitt, Philip. 1995. On a screen near you: Cyberporn. *Time* 27 [Australia] (July 10): 48–55.

Epstein, Robert. 1992. The quest for the thinking computer. *AI Magazine* 13 (Summer): 81–95.

Evans, Christopher. 1992. Can a machine think? In *Philosophy and Contemporary Issues*. 6th ed. Ed. John R. Burr and Milton Goldinger. New York: Macmillan, pp. 423–35.

Feigenbaum, Edward A. 1996. Turing award lecture: How the "What" became the "How." *Communications of the ACM* 39 (May): 97–104.

Feinberg, Joel. 1970. *Doing and Deserving: Essays in the Theory of Responsibility*. Princeton, NJ: Princeton University Press.

Feinberg, Joel. 1983. *The Moral Limits of the Criminal Law*. 4 vols. New York: Oxford University Press.

Ford, George, and Sylvere Monod, eds. 1966. *Charles Dickens: Hard Times*. An authoritative text, backgrounds, sources, and contemporary reactions criticisms. New York: W. W. Norton & Company.

Forester, Tom. 1990. Software theft and the problem of intellectual property rights. *Computers and Society* 20 (March): 2–11.

Forester, Tom, and Perry Morrison. 1995. *Computer Ethics: Cautionary Tales and Ethical Dilemmas in Computing*. 2d ed. Cambridge, MA: MIT Press.

Foskett, D. J. 1962. *The Creed of a Librarian: No Politics, No Religion, No Morals*. London: Library Association.

Fullinwider, Robert. 1995. Professional codes and moral understanding. *Res Publica* 4: 1–6.

Giles, Richard. 1990. Are there times when censorship is justified? In *For and against: Public Issues in Australia*, ed. Richard Giles. Milton, Qld: Brooks Waterloo, p. 61.

Goble, John C., Ken Hinckley, Randy Pausch, John W. Snell, and Neal F. Kassell. 1995. Two-handed spatial interface tools for neurosurgical planning. *Computer* 28 (July): 20–26.

Goldman, Alan H. 1980. *The Moral Foundations of Professional Ethics*. Baltimore, MD: Rowman & Littlefield.

Goranzon, B. 1988. The practice of the use of computers. A paradoxical encounter between different traditions of knowledge. In *Knowledge, Skill and Artificial Intelligence*, ed. Bo Goranzon and Ingela Josefson. London: Springer-Verlag, pp. 9–18.

Grassian, Victor. 1981. *Moral Reasoning: Ethical Theory and Some Contemporary Moral Problems*. Englewood Cliffs, NJ: Prentice Hall.

Grosch, Herb. 1994. Dehumanization in the workplace. *Communications of the ACM* 37 (November): 122.

Hadfield, Greg, and Mark Skipworth. 1993a. Private lives for sale in illicit info-market. *Sunday Times* (London), 18 July.

Hadfield, Greg, and Mark Skipworth. 1993b. Firms keep "dirty data" on sex lives of staff. *Sunday Times* (London), 25 July.

Haugeland, John. 1987. *Artificial Intelligence: The Very Idea.* Cambridge, MA: MIT Press.

Hauptman, Robert. 1976. Professionalism or culpability? An experiment in ethics. *Wilson Library Bulletin* 50: 626–27.

Hauptman, Robert. 1988. *Ethical Challenges in Librarianship.* Phoenix, AZ: Oryx Press.

Hettinger, Edwin C. 1989. Justifying intellectual property. *Philosophy and Public Affairs* 18: 31–52.

Hobbes, Thomas. 1651. *Leviathan;* edition of Macpherson, 1975.

Hodges, Larry F., Rob Kooper, Thomas C. Meyer, Barbara O. Rothbaum, Dan Opdyke, Johannes J. de Graaff, James S. Williford, and Max M. North. 1995. Virtual environments for treating the fear of heights. *Computer* 28 (July): 27–34.

Hume, David. 1739. *A Treatise of Human Nature;* edition of Selby-Bigge, 1975.

Johnson, Deborah G. 1994. *Computer Ethics.* 2d ed. Englewood Cliffs, NJ: Prentice Hall.

Johnson, Deborah G., and John M. Mulvey. 1995. Accountability and computer decision support systems. *Communications of the ACM* 38 (December): 58–64.

Johnson, Deborah G., and Helen F. Nissenbaum, eds. 1994. *Computers, Ethics and Social Values.* Englewood Cliffs, NJ: Prentice Hall.

Johnson-Laird, P. N. 1988. *The Computer and the Mind: An Introduction to Cognitive Science.* London: Fontana Press.

Jordan, Z. A., ed. 1971. *Karl Marx: Economy, Class and Social Revolution.* London: Nelson.

Katz, William A. 1992. *Introduction to Reference Work Volume 2: Reference Services and Reference Processes.* 6th ed. New York: McGraw-Hill.

Kizza, Joseph M., ed. 1994. *Ethics in the Computer Age: Conference Proceedings, Gatlinburg, Tennessee, November 11–13, 1994.* New York: Association for Computing Machinery.

Kizza, Joseph M., ed. 1996. *The Social and Ethical Issues of the Computer Revolution.* Jefferson, NC: McFarland and Company.

Kuhl, Jon, Douglas Evans, Yiannis Papelis, Richard Romano, and Ginger Watson. 1995. The Iowa simulator: An immersive research environment. *Computer* 28 (July): 42–48.

Kultgen, John. 1988. *Ethics and Professionalism.* Philadelphia: University of Pennsylvania Press.

Kurzweil, Raymond. 1990. *The Age of Intelligent Machines.* Cambridge, MA: MIT Press.

Larijani, L. Casey. 1994. *The Virtual Reality Primer.* New York: McGraw Hill.

Laslett, Peter, ed. 1965. *John Locke, Two Treatises of Government. A Critical Edition with an Introduction and Apparatus Criticus.* New York: New American Library.

Leinfuss, Emily. 1995. Marketing myths. *Information Age* [Melbourne, Australia] (July): 16.

Level 5 Object for Microsoft Windows. Release 2.5, 1992. New York: Information Builders.

Leveson, Nancy G. 1991. Software safety in embedded computer systems. *Communications of the ACM* 34 (February): 34–46.

Littlewood, Bev, and Lorenzo Strigini. 1992. The risks of software. *Scientific American* 267 (November): 38–43.

Locke, John. 1689. *Second Treatise of Government*; edition of Laslett, 1965.

Long, Robert Emmet, ed. 1990. *Censorship*. The Reference Shelf, vol. 62, no. 3. New York: H. W. Wilson.

Mackie, J. L. 1977. *Ethics: Inventing Right and Wrong*. Harmondsworth: Penguin Books.

MacNeil, Heather. 1992. *Without Consent: The Ethics of Disclosing Personal Information in Public Archives*. Metuchen, NJ: Scarecrow Press.

Macpherson, C. B., ed. 1975. *Thomas Hobbes: Leviathan*. Harmondsworth: Penguin Books.

Malone, K., and A. C. Baugh. 1967. *The Middle Ages*. London: Routledge & Kegan Paul.

Marx, Karl. 1844. *Ecomonic and Philosophical Manuscripts*; edition of Z. A. Jordan, 1971.

Marx, Karl, and Friedrich Engels. 1848. *Manifesto of the Communist Party*; 1971 edition, Moscow: Progress Publishers.

Matthews, Robert. 1994. Computers at the dawn of creativity. *New Scientist* 144 (10 December): 30–34.

May, Larry, and Stacy Hoffman, eds. 1991. *Collective Responsibility: Five Decades of Debate in Theoretical and Applied Ethics*. Baltimore, MD: Rowman and Littlefield.

McCalman, Janet. 1995. Copyright and scholarship: Why it matters for academics. Unpublished paper, Melbourne.

McFarland, Michael C. 1990. Urgency of ethical standards intensifies in computer community. *Computer* 23 (March): 77–81.

McIntosh, Trudi. 1995. Privacy issue to dominate '90s. *The Australian*, 14 March.

Mill, John Stuart. 1859. *On Liberty*; page citations to the edition of David Spitz, 1975.

Mill, John Stuart. 1863. *Utilitarianism*; edition of Sokar Piest, 1957.

Miller, Seumas. 1996. Privacy, databases and computers. *Australian Library Review* 13 (February): 60–64.

Million, Angela C., and Kim N. Fisher. 1986. Library records: A review of confidentiality laws and policies. *Journal of Academic Librarianship* 11: 346–49.

Mills, J. J. 1992. *Information Resources and Services in Australia*. 2d ed. Wagga Wagga: Centre for Information Studies.

Minsky, M. L., ed. 1968. *Semantic Information Processing*. Cambridge, Mass: MIT Press.

Mitchell, William J. 1994. When is seeing believing? *Scientific American* (February): 44–49.

Moore, James H. 1985. What is computer ethics? *Metaphilosophy* 16: 266–75.

Neumann, Peter G. 1990. Some reflections on a telephone switching problem. *Communications of the ACM* 33 (January): 154.

Nissenbaum, Helen. 1994. Computing and accountability. *Communications of the ACM* 37 (January): 73–80.

Northmore, David. 1990. *Freedom of Information Handbook*. London: Bloomsbury.

Nozick, Robert. 1980. *Anarchy, State, and Utopia*. Oxford: Blackwell.

Nussbaum, Karen. 1991. Computer monitoring: A threat to the right to privacy? In *Ethical Issues in Information Systems*, ed. Roy Dejoie, George Fowler, and David Paradice. Boston: Boyd & Fraser, 134–39.

Orr, Lisa, ed. 1990. *Censorship: Opposing Viewpoints*. San Diego, CA: Greenhaven Press.

Oz, Effy. 1994. *Ethics for the Information Age*. [no place]: Business and Educational Technologies.

Panteli, Nick, and Martin Corbett. 1995. Deskilling (1974–1994): 20 years after— in the era of empowerment. *Ethicomp 95: An International Conference on the Ethical Issues of Using Information Technology. Proceedings*. Vol. 1, unpaginated.

Parnas, David L., A. John van Schouwen, and Shu Po Kwan. 1990. Evaluation of safety-critical software. *Communications of the ACM* 33 (June): 636–48.

Pennock, J., and J. Chapman, eds. 1971. *Nomos XIII: Privacy*. New York: Atherton Press.

Piest, Sokar, ed. 1957. *John Stuart Mill: Utilitarianism*. New York: Liberal Arts Press.

Pimentel, Ken, and Kevin Texeira. 1993. *Virtual Reality: Through the New Looking Glass*. New York: McGraw Hill.

Pratt, David R., Michael Zyda, and Kristen Kelleher. 1995. Virtual reality: In the mind of the beholder. *Computer* (July):17–18.

Rachels, James. 1986. *The Elements of Moral Philosophy*. New York: Random House.

Rawls, John. 1972. *A Theory of Justice*. Oxford: Oxford University Press.

Reddy Raj. 1996. Turing award lecture: To dream the impossible dream. *Communications of the ACM* 39 (May): 105–13.

Rheingold, H. 1991. *Virtual Reality*. London: Secker & Warburg.

Rich, Elaine, and Kevin Knight. 1991. *Artificial Intelligence*. 2d ed. New York: McGraw-Hill.

Roberts, Norman, and Tania Konn. 1990. *Librarians and Professional Status: Continuing Professional Development and Academic Libraries*. London: The Library Association.

Russell, Anne M. 1994. Four Predictions: Who will win and who will lose, and will digital art ever get better? *American Photo* 5 (May/June): 58–59.

Samuelson, Pamela. 1990. Should program algorithms be patented? *Communications of the ACM* 33 (August): 23–27.

Samuelson, Pamela. 1992. Copyright law and electronic compilations of data. *Communications of the ACM* 35 (February): 27–32.

Samuelson, Pamela. 1993a. Liability for defective electronic information. *Communications of the ACM* 36 (January): 21–26.

Samuelson, Pamela. 1993b. Computer programs and copyright's fair use doctrine. *Communications of the ACM* 36 (September): 19–25.

Samuelson, Pamela. 1994. Copyright's fair use doctrine and digital data. *Communications of the ACM* 37 (January): 21–27.

Samuelson, Pamela. 1995. Copyright and digital libraries. *Communications of the ACM* 38 (April): 15–21, 110.

Scott, Jan, and John Weckert. 1996. Expert system explanation: A methodology for generation. In *Critical Technology: Proceedings of the Third World Congress on Expert Systems*, ed. Jae Kyu Lee, Jay Liebowitz, and Young Moon Chae. New York: Cognizant Communication Corporation, pp. 569–76.

Searle, John R. 1980. Minds, brains, and programs. *The Behavioral and Brain Sciences* 3: 417–24.

Searle, John R. 1984. *Minds, Brains, and Science*. London: British Broadcasting Corporation.

Selby-Bigge, L. A., ed. 1975. *Hume's Treatise of Human Nature*. Oxford: Clarendon Press.

Shaver, Donna B., Nancy S. Hewison, and Leslie W. Wykoff. 1985. Ethics for online intermediaries. *Special Libraries* 76 (Fall): 238–45.

Sidgwick, Henry. 1874. *The Methods of Ethics*. 1966 ed. New York: Dover Publications.

Singer, Peter. 1993. *How Are We to Live? Ethics in an Age of Self-Interest*. Melbourne: Text Publishing Company.

Singer, Peter, ed. 1994. *Ethics*. Oxford: Oxford University Press.

Snizek, William E. 1995. Virtual offices: Some neglected considerations. *Communications of the ACM* 38 (September): 15–17.

Spinnello, Richard A. 1995. *Ethical Aspects of Information Technology*. Englewood Cliffs, NJ: Prentice Hall, chapter 6.

Spitz, David, ed. 1975. *John Stuart Mill, On Liberty: Annotated Text, Sources and Background Criticism*. New York: W. W. Norton & Company.

Spring, Michael B. 1995. The virtual library. *Fantastic Futures: Virtual and in the Flesh*. National reference and information services conference, September 13–15. Presented by the Reference and Information Services Section of ALIA (RAISS).

Steidlmeier, Paul. 1992. *People and Profits: The Ethics of Capitalism*. Englewood Cliffs, NJ: Prentice Hall.

Sunday Age [Melbourne, Australia], 7 January 1996.

Talbott, Stephen L. 1995. *The Future Does Not Compute: Transcending the Machines in Our Midst*. Sebastopol, CA: O'Reilly & Associates.

Tavani, Herman T. 1995. A computer ethics bibliography. *Computers and Society* 25 (June): 8–18; (September): 27–37; (December): 9–38.

Ten, C. L. 1980. *Mill on Liberty*. Oxford: Clarendon Press.

Thomson, J. A. K. 1971. *The Ethics of Aristotle. The Nicomachean Ethics Translated*. Harmondsworth: Penguin Books.

Turing, A. M. 1950. Computing machinery and intelligence. *Mind* 59: 433–60.

"The Universal Declaration of Human Rights." *Human Rights Manual*. 1993. Canberra: Australian Government Publishing Service, pp. 137–42.

Waldron, Jeremy. 1979. Enough and as good left for others. *Philosophical Quarterly* 29: 319–28.

Weckert, John, and Stuart Ferguson. 1993. Ethics, reference librarians and expert systems. *Australian Library Journal* 42 (August): 172–81.

Weil, Vivian, and John Snapper, eds. 1989. *Owning Scientific and Technical Information*. New Brunswick, NJ: Rutgers University Press.

Weizenbaum, Joseph. 1976. ELIZA—A computer program for the study of natural language communication between man and machine. *Communications of the ACM* 9 (January): 36–45.

Weizenbaum, Joseph. 1984. *Computer Power and Human Reason: From Judgement to Calculation*. Harmondsworth: Penguin Books.

Wexelblat, Alan, ed. 1993. *Virtual Reality: Applications and Explorations*. Boston: Academic Press Professional.

Wiener, Paul B. 1983. Is it ethical to help a student find a how-to-commit-suicide manual, and is that all you do? *American Libraries* 14: 643.

Wiener, Paul B. 1987. Mad bombers and ethical librarians: A dialogue with Robert Hauptman and John Swan. *Catholic Library World* 58: 161–63.

Yourdon, Edward. 1995. When good enough software is best. *IEEE Software* 12 (May): 79–81.

Index

About the Authors

JOHN WECKERT is Senior Lecturer in Information Technology at Charles Sturt University in Australia. He has an M.A. from La Trobe University and a Ph.D. from the University of Melbourne. His main teaching and research interests are in the field of artificial intelligence, especially knowledge-based systems, and computer ethics.

DOUGLAS ADENEY is Lecturer in Philosophy at the University of Melbourne. He has an M.A. from Monash University and a Ph.D from the University of St. Andrews. His main teaching and research interests are in moral and political philosophy, and he additionally enjoys teaching in the areas of general metaphysics and logic.

ISBN 0-313-29362-7

90000>

EAN

9 780313 293627

HARDCOVER BAR CODE